COLORING BOOK FOR TEENS AND YOUNG ADULTS

Stilettos and Boots

Stilettos and Boots

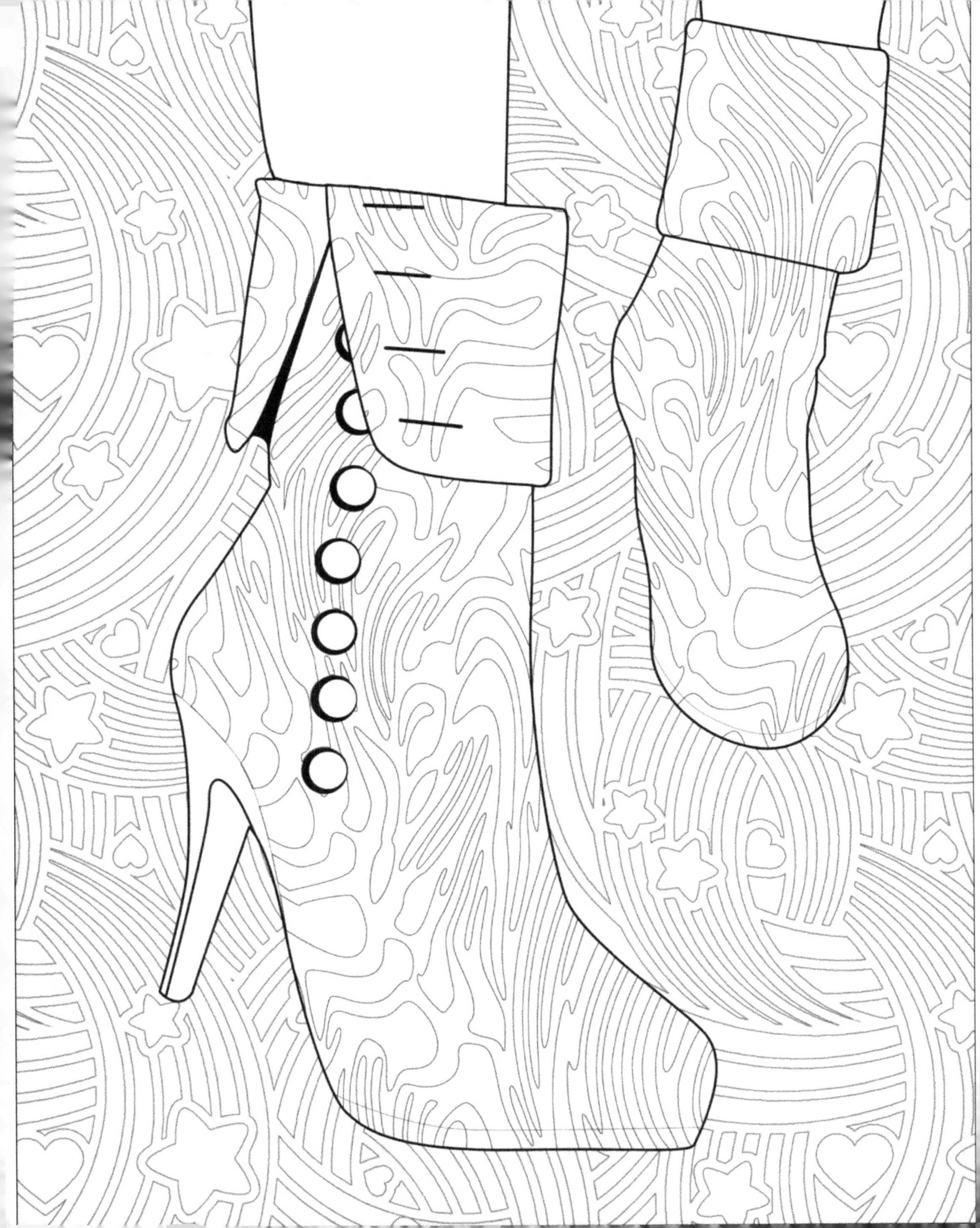

Stilettos and Boots

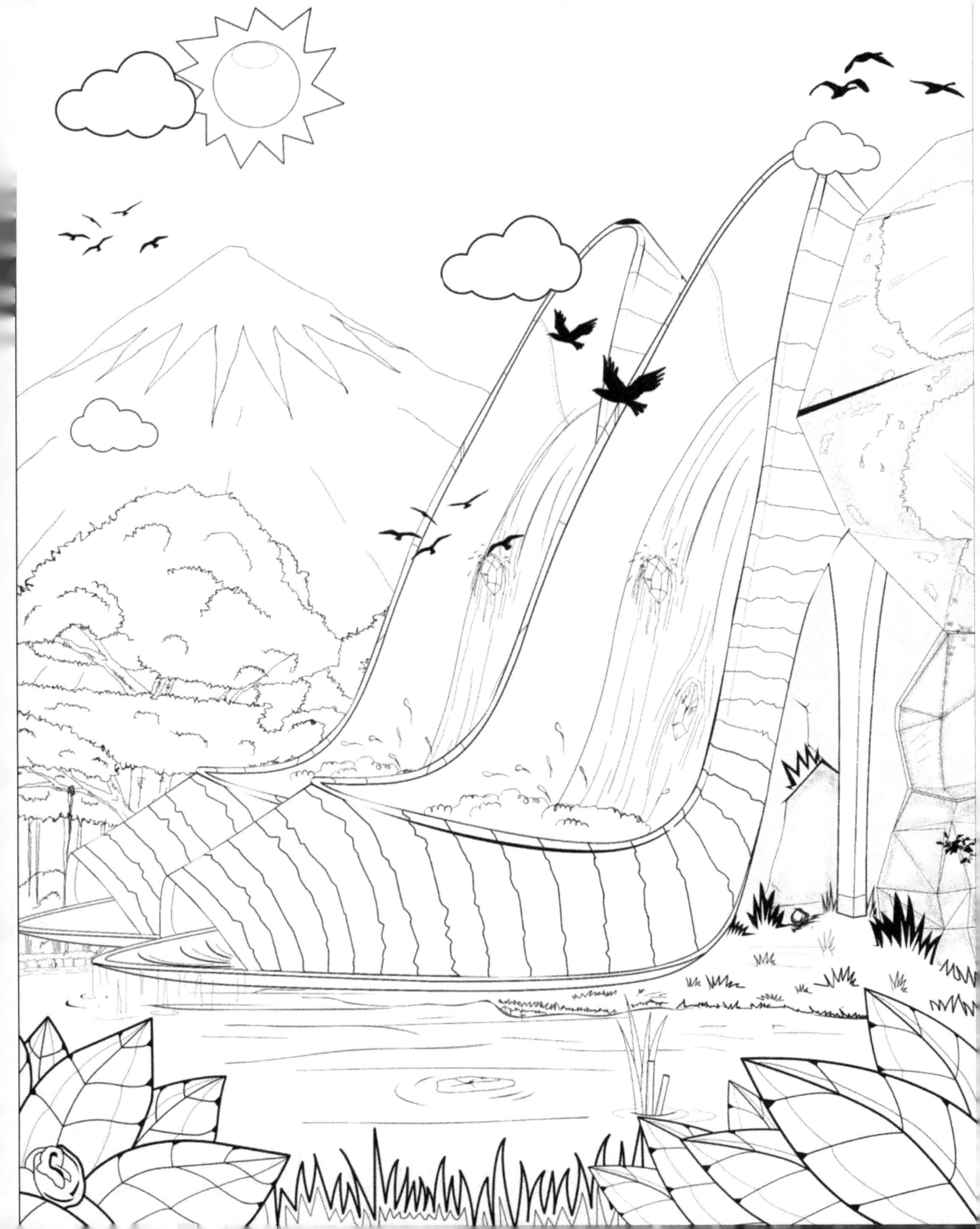

Stilettos and Boots

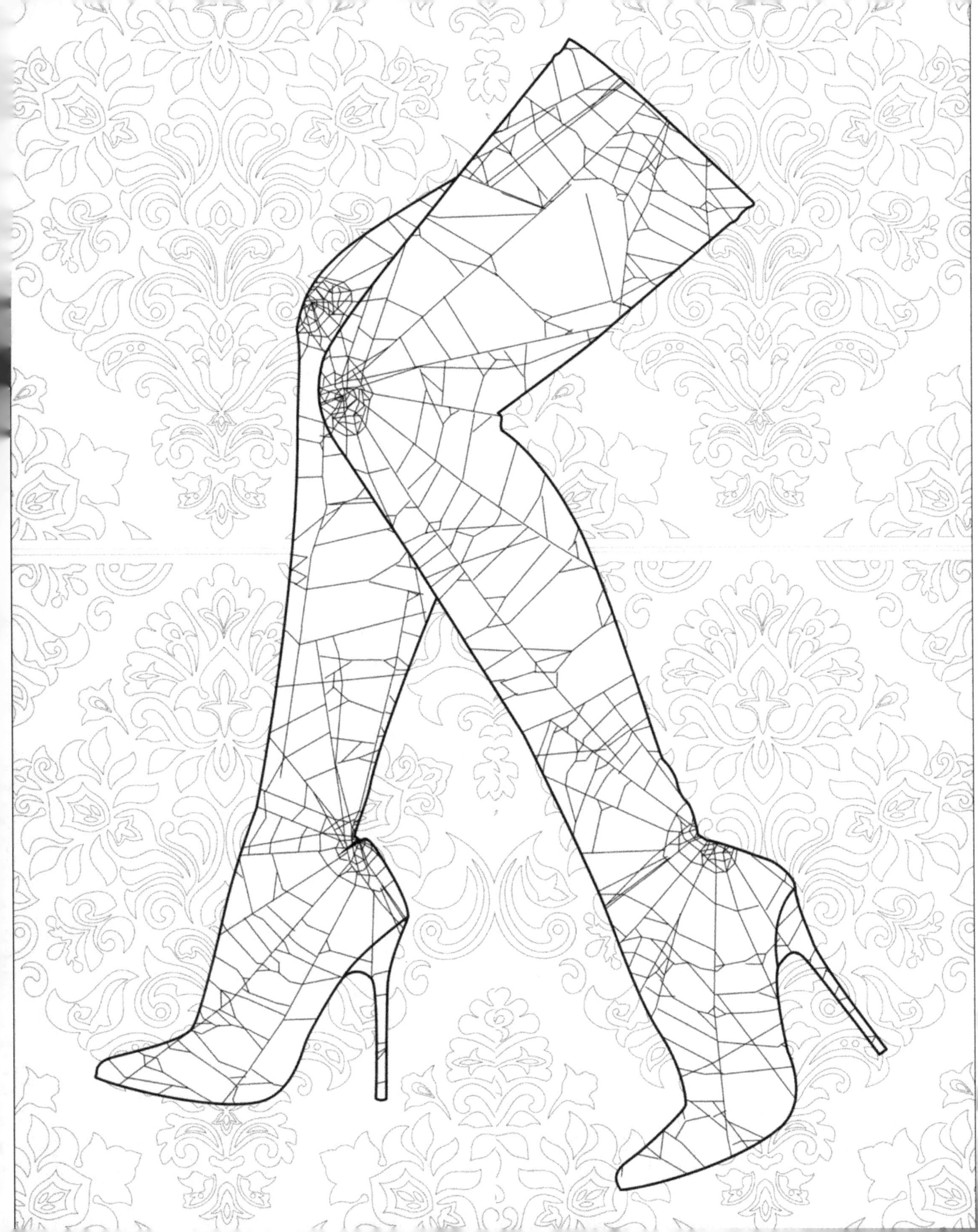

Stilettos and Boots

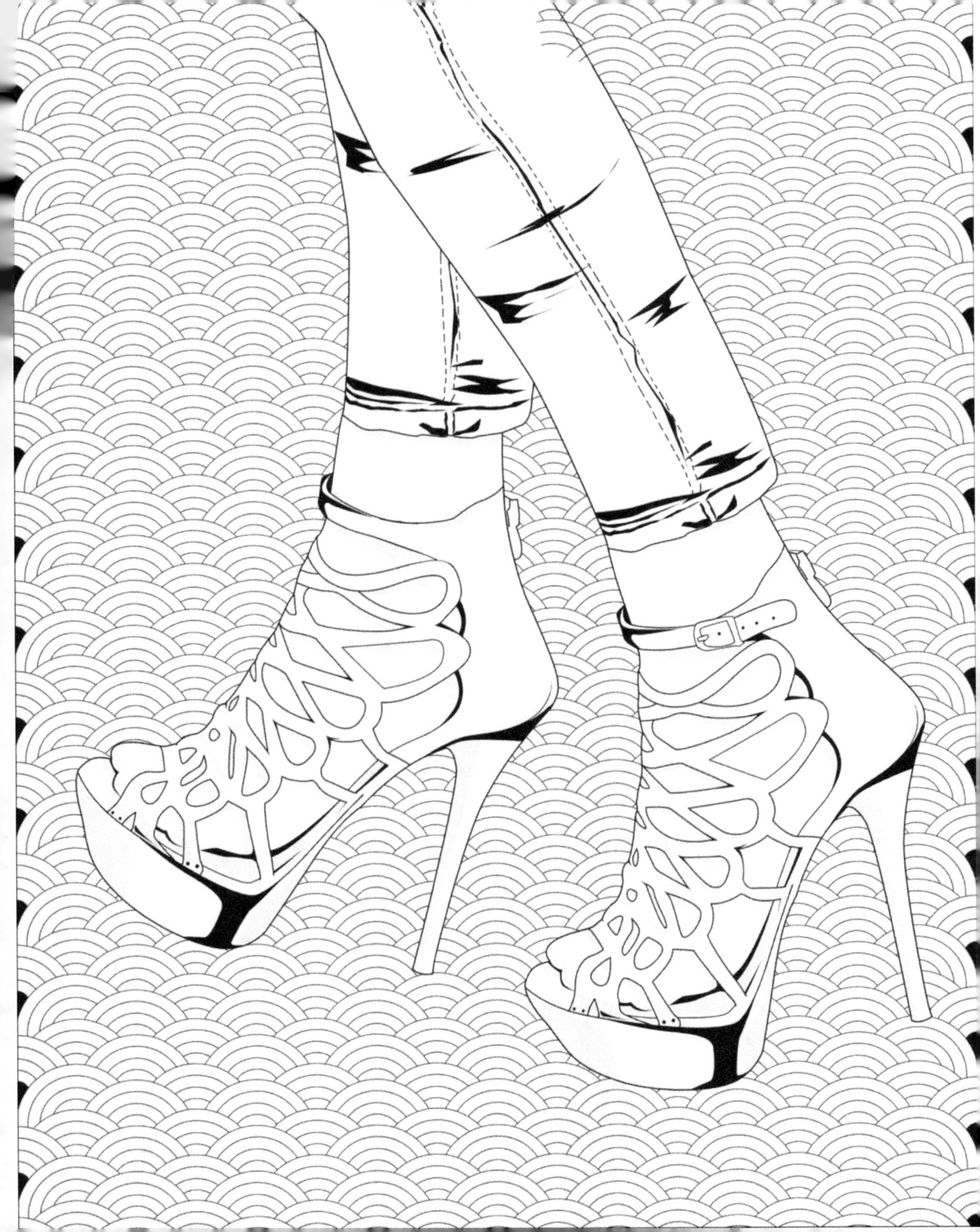

Stilettos and Boots

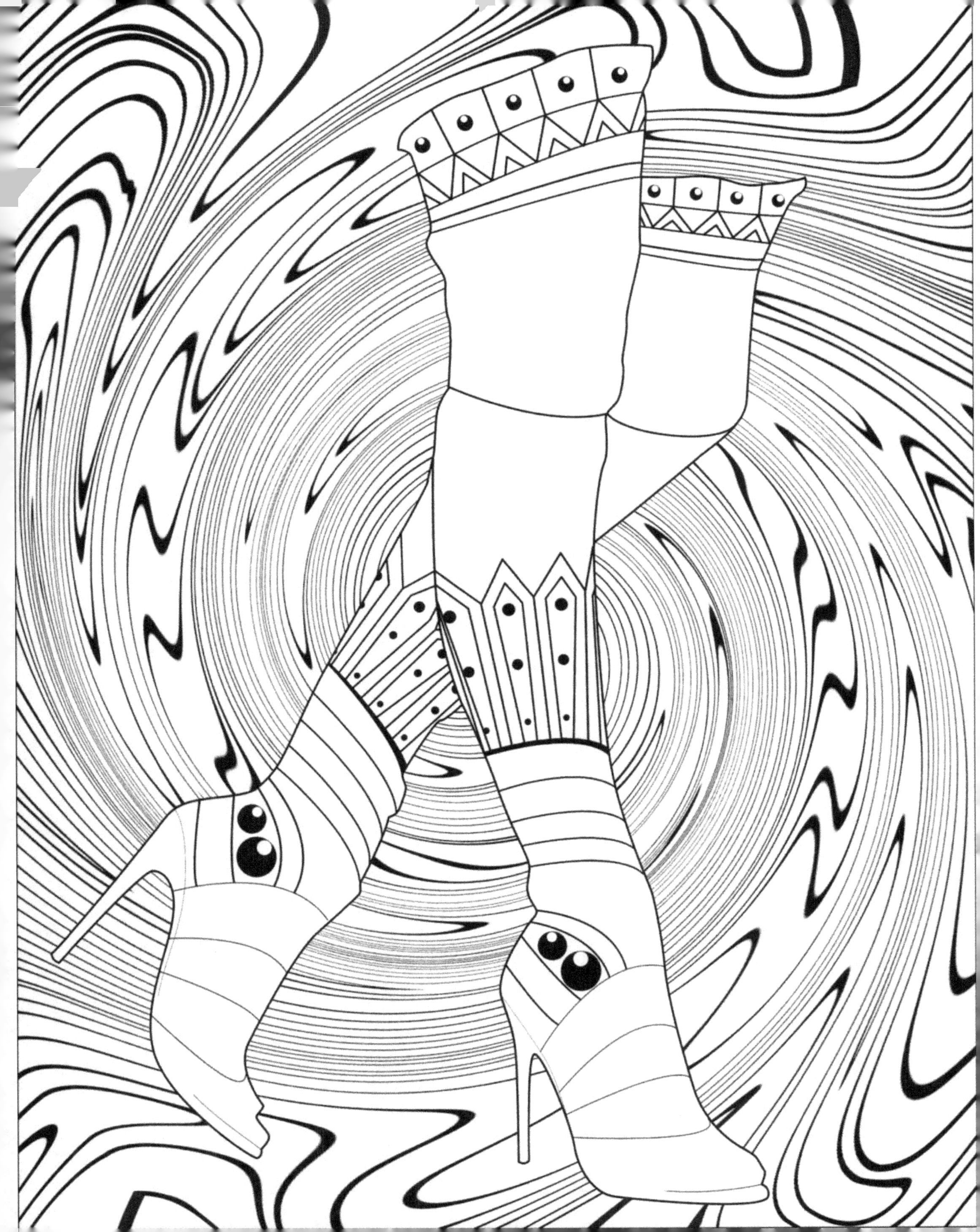

Stilettos and Boots

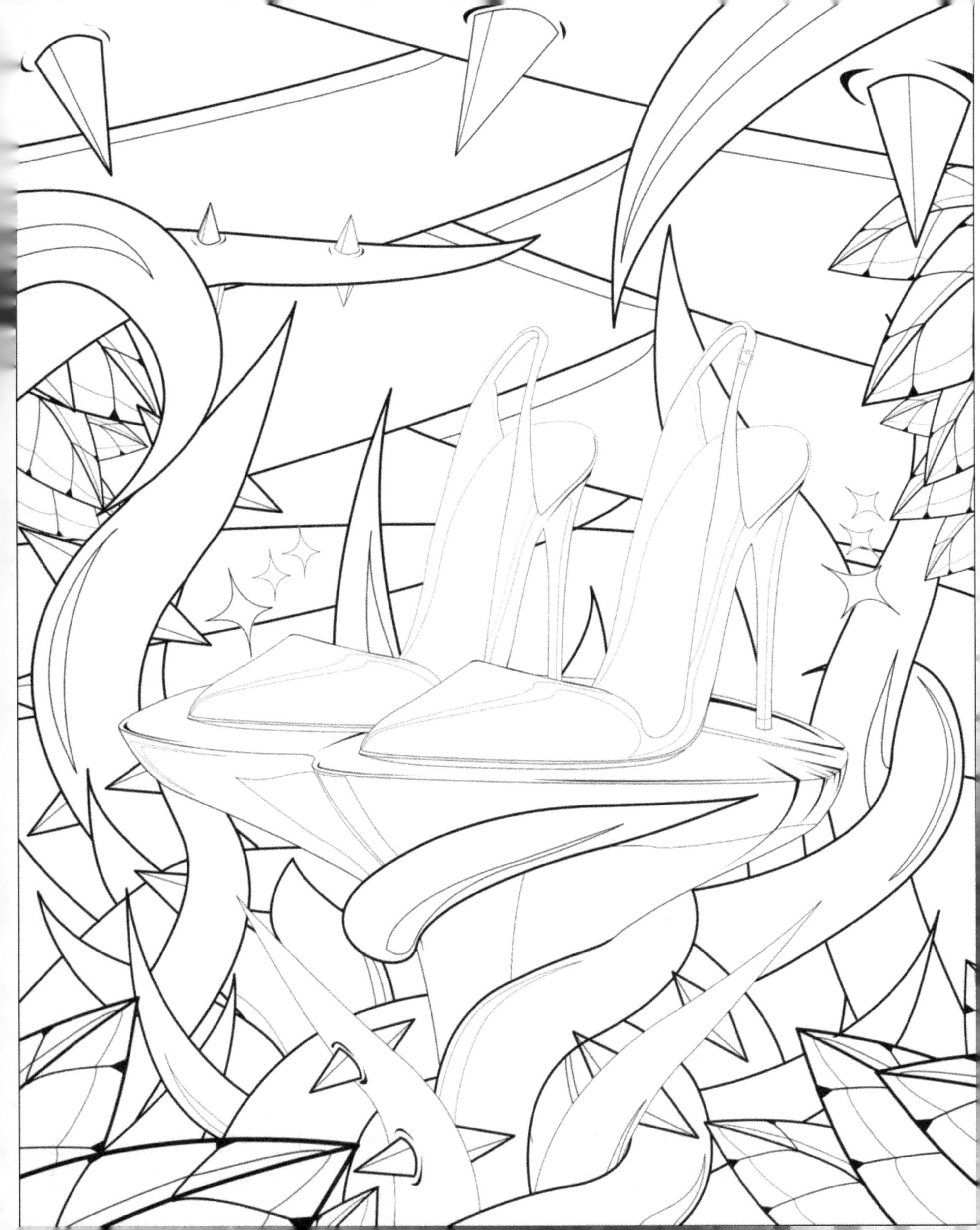

Stilettos and Boots

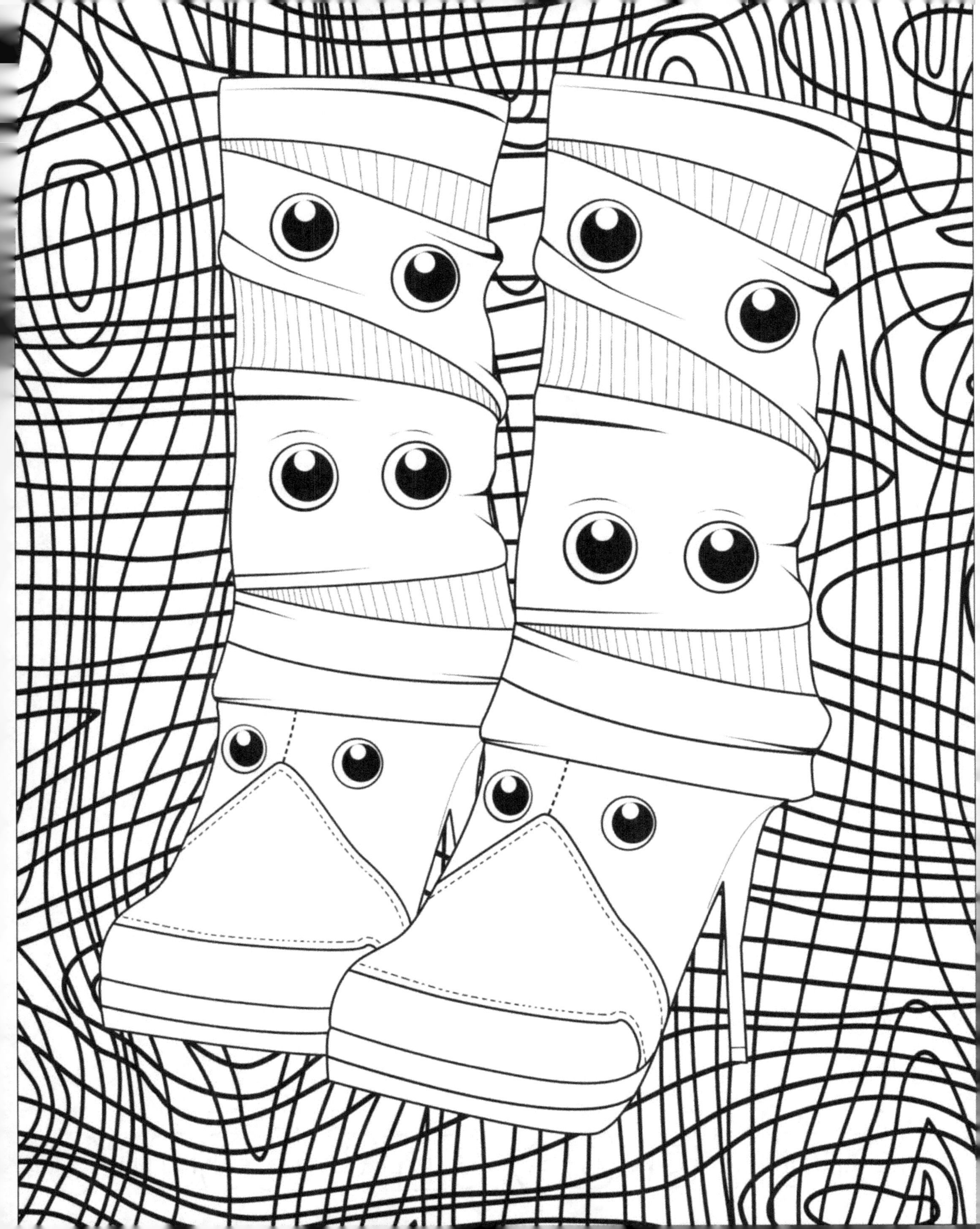

Stilettos and Boots

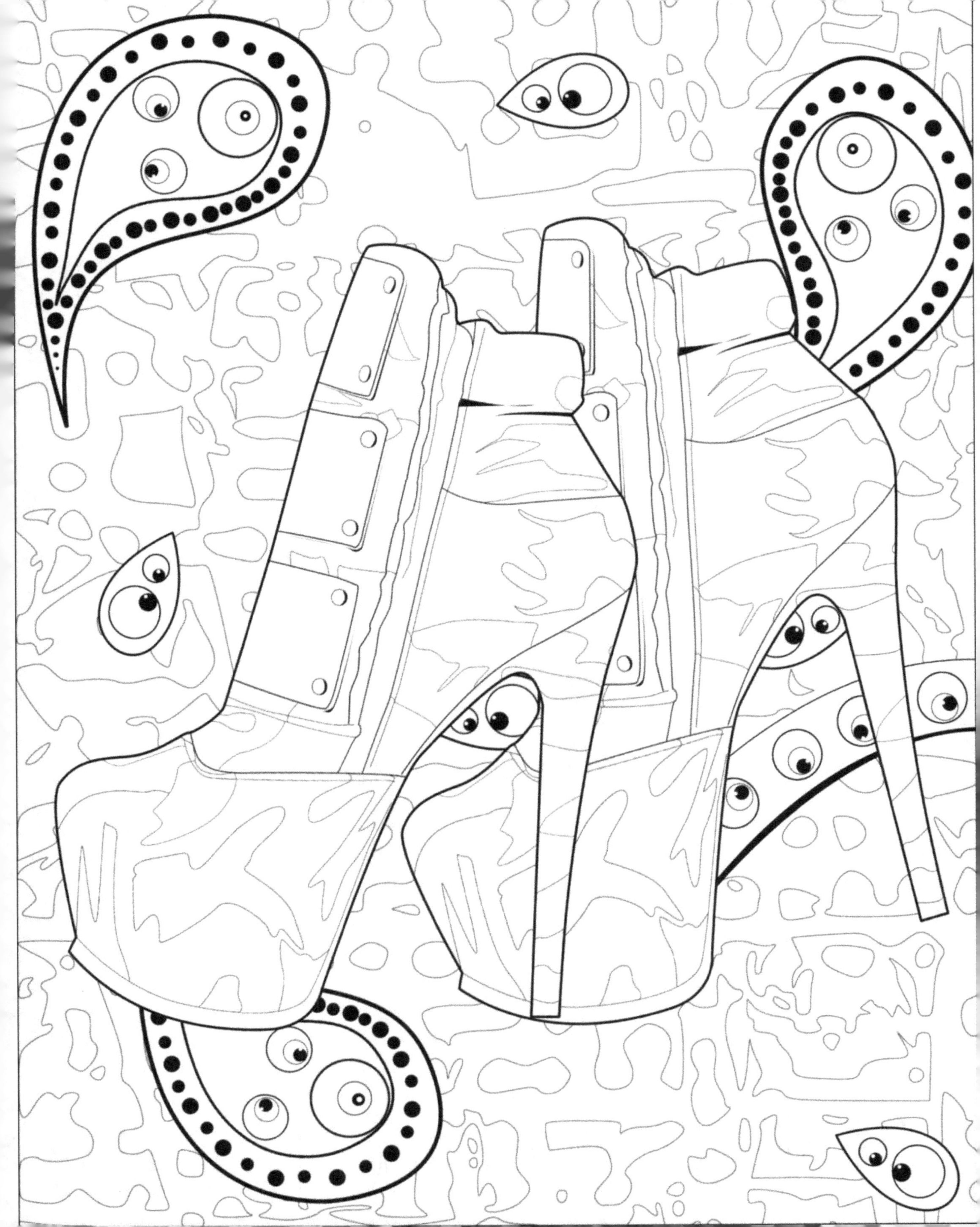

Stilettos and Boots

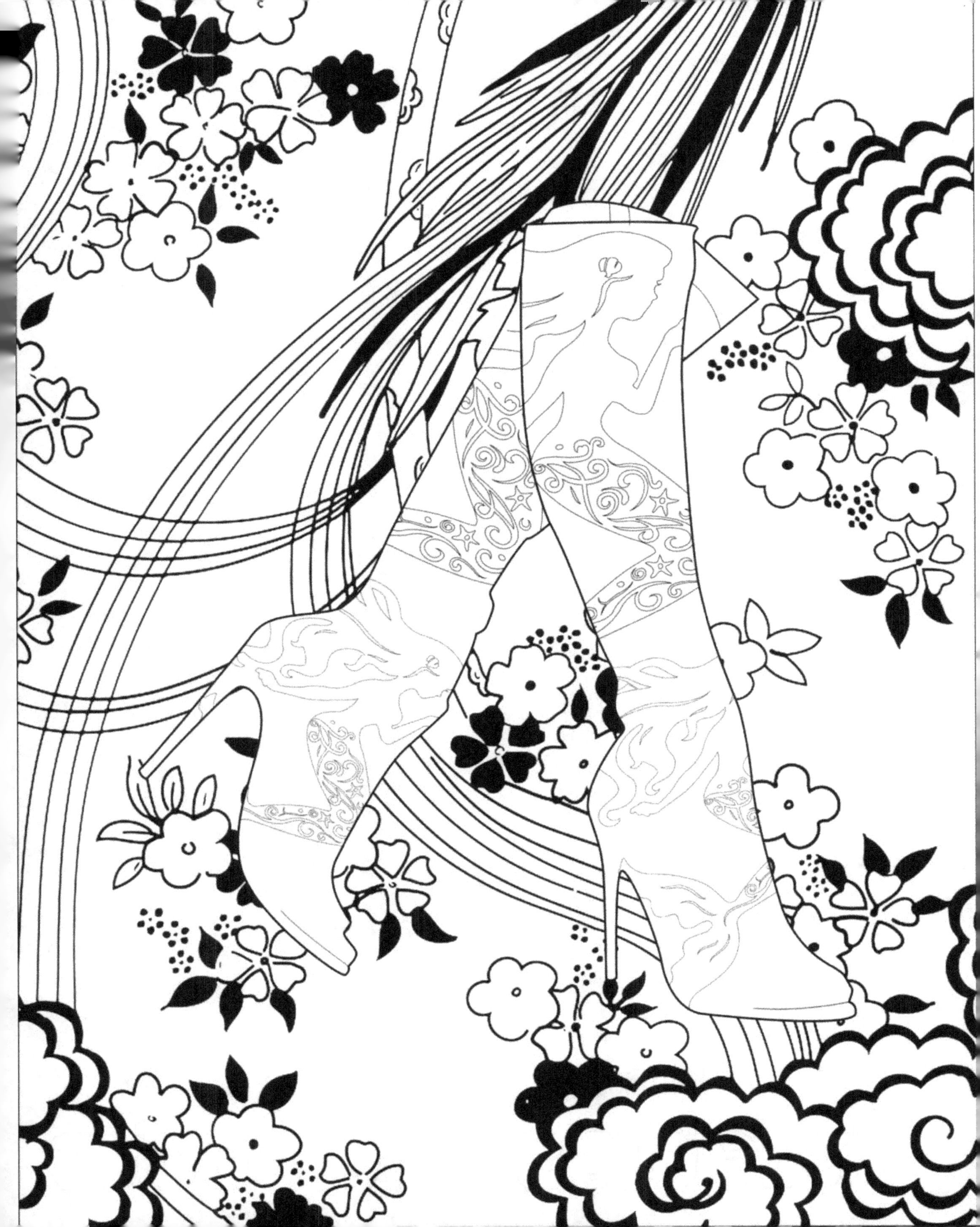

Stilettos and Boots

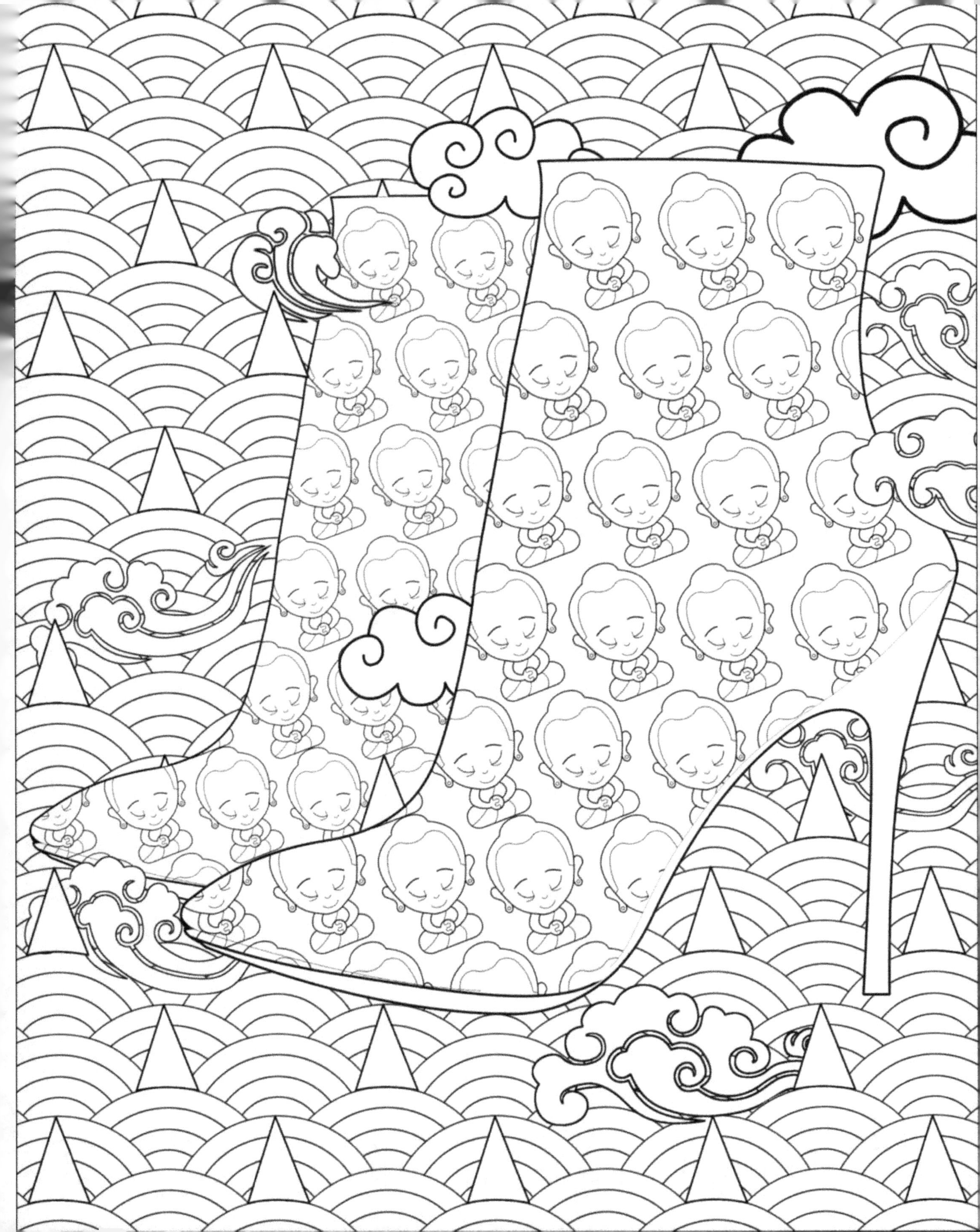

Stilettos and Boots

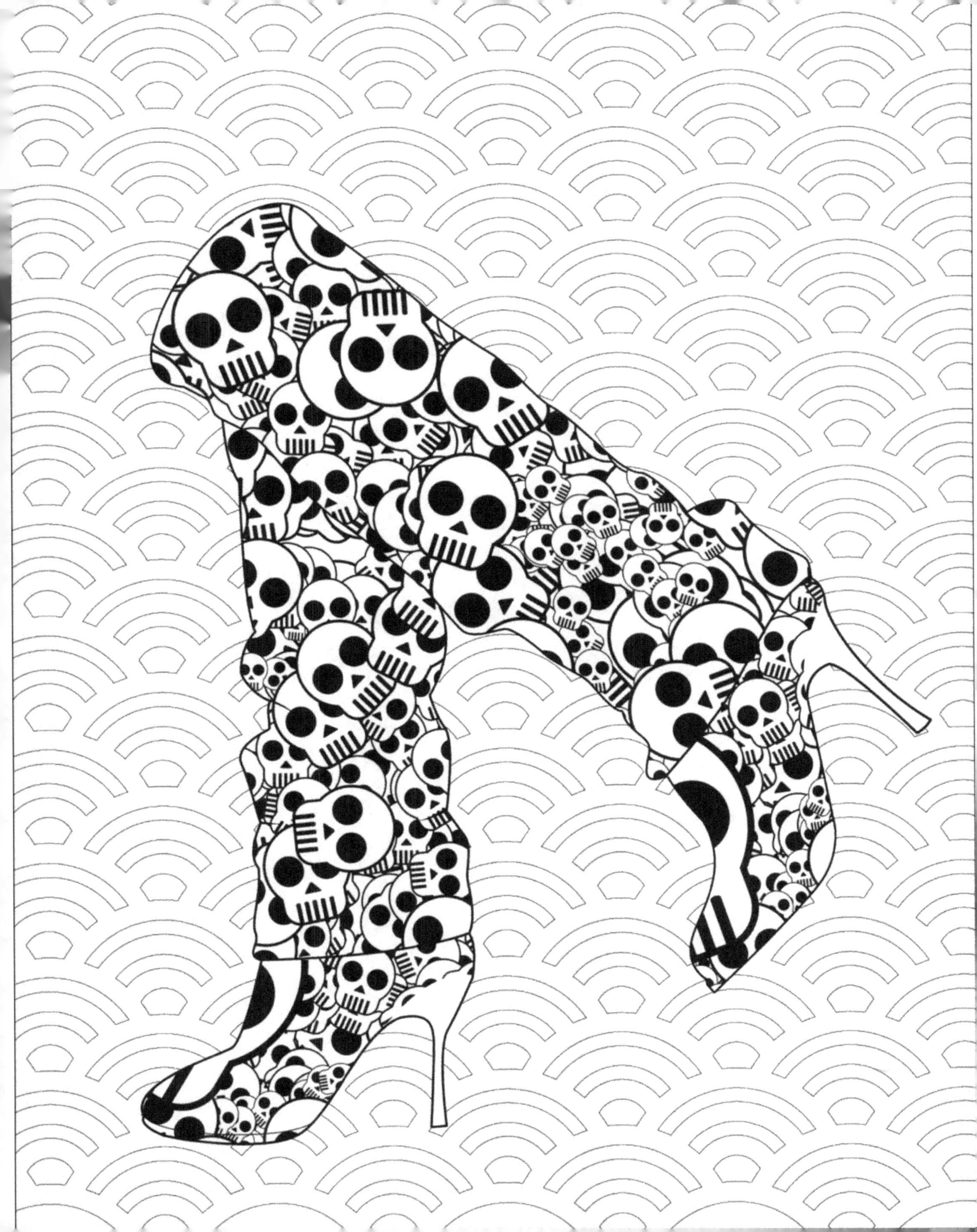

Stilettos and Boots

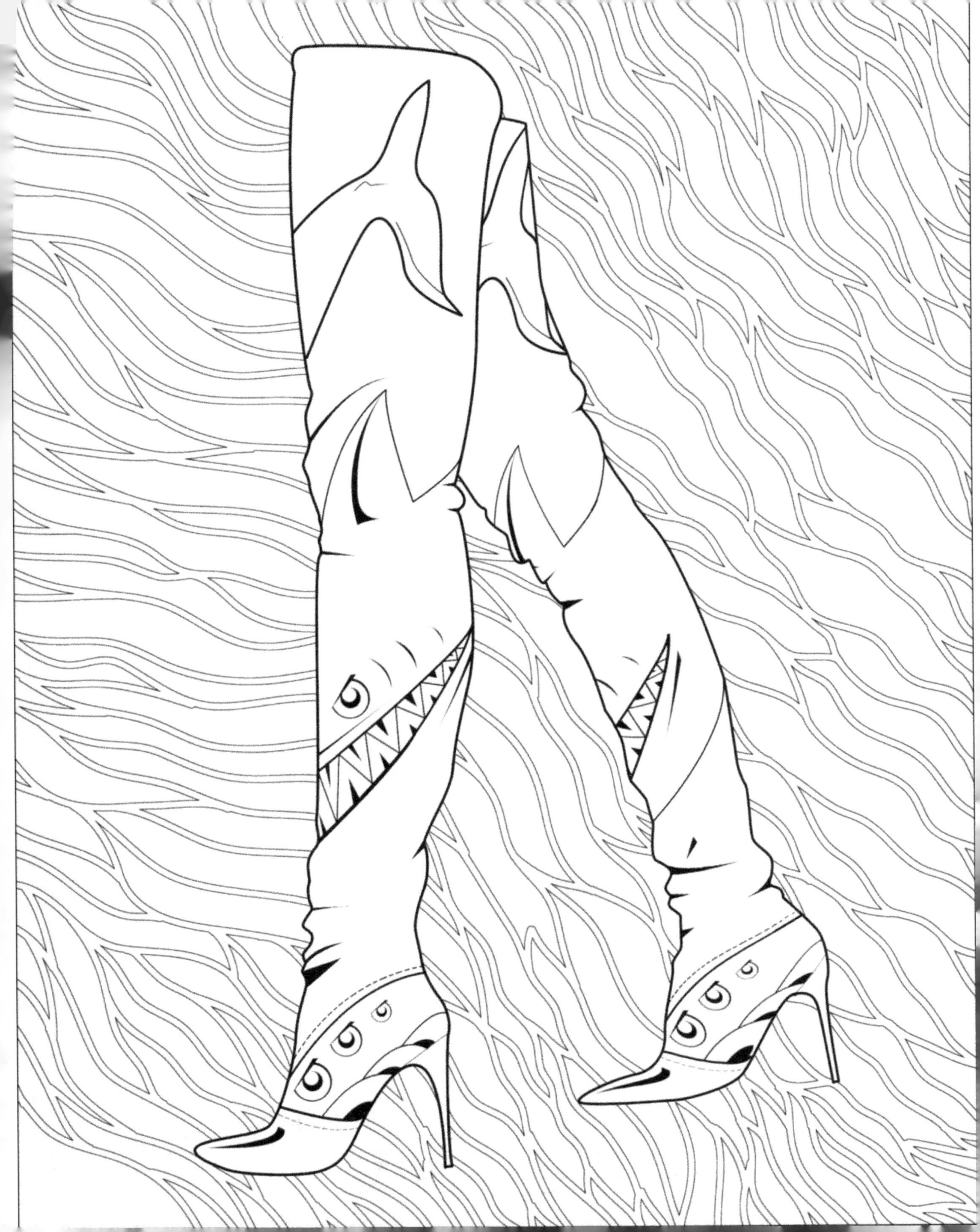

Stilettos and Boots

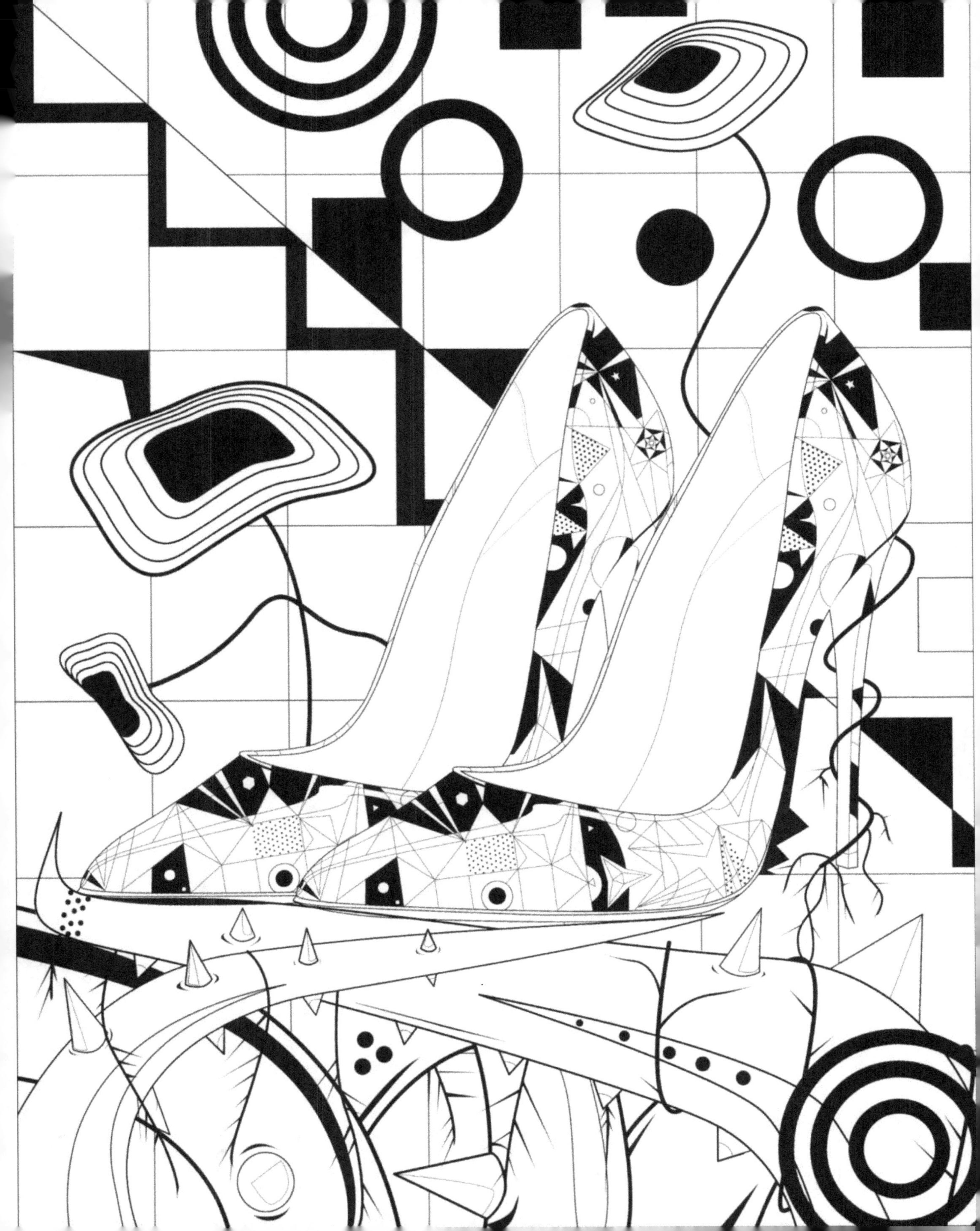

Stilettos and Boots

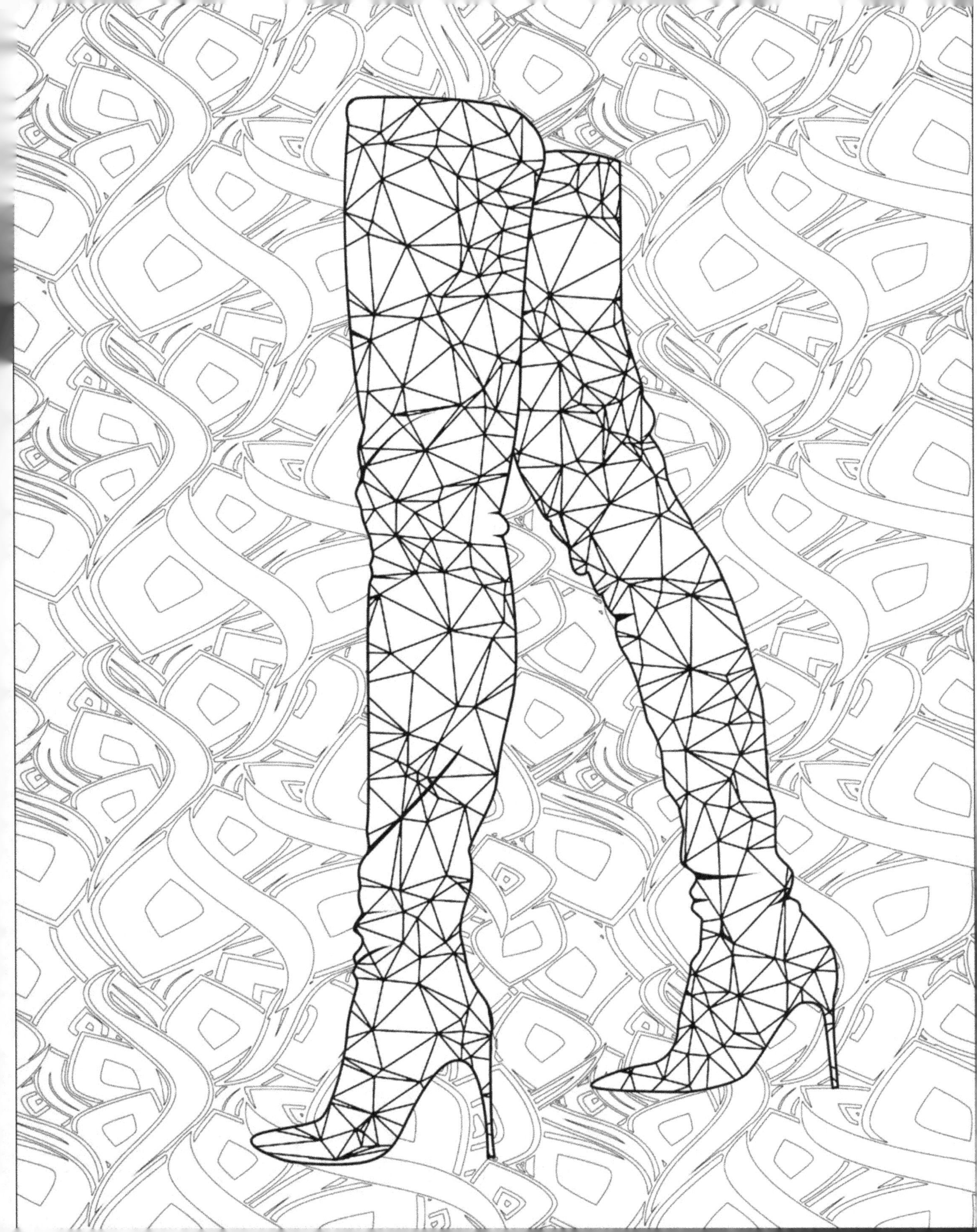

Stilettos and Boots

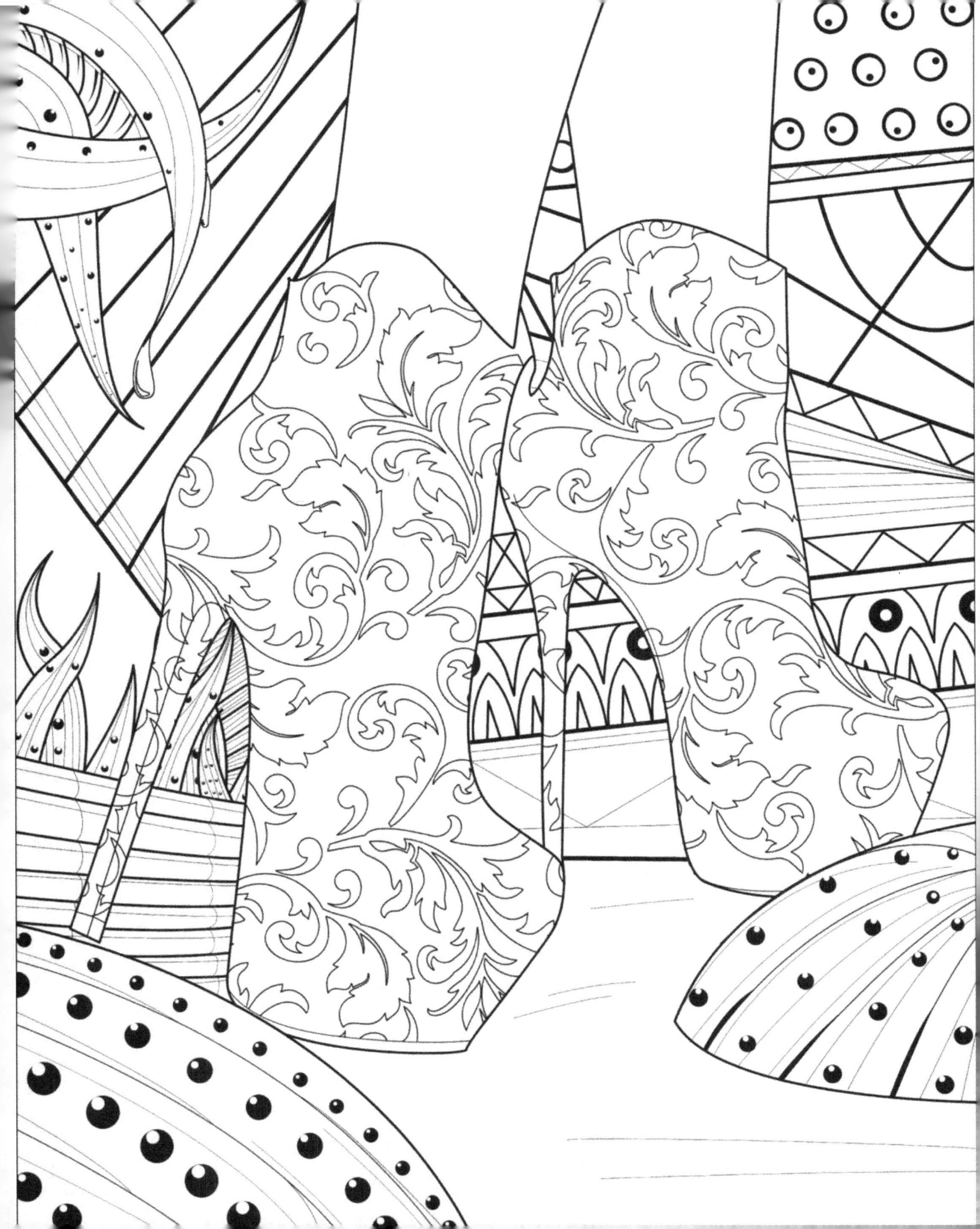

Stilettos and Boots

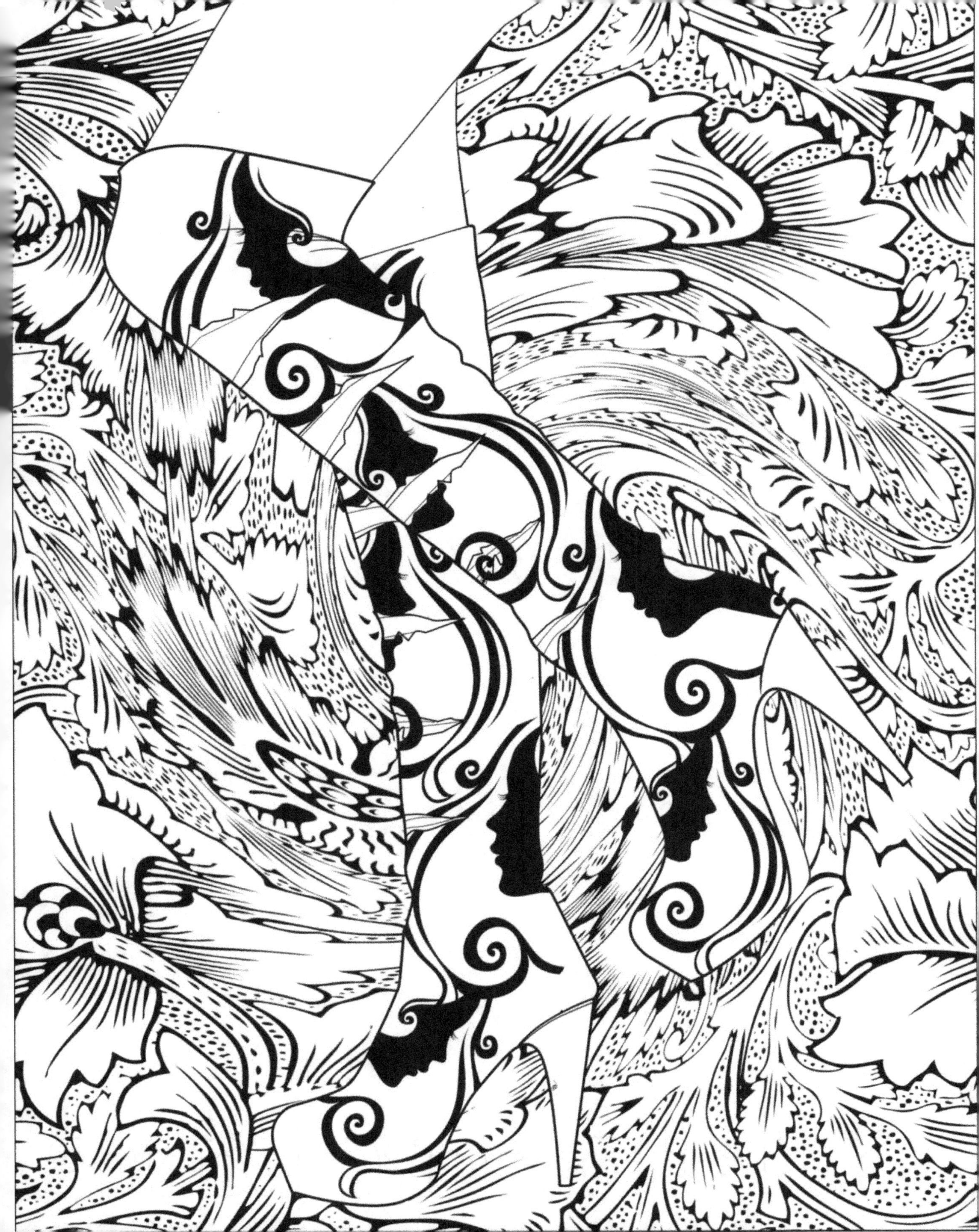

Stilettos and Boots

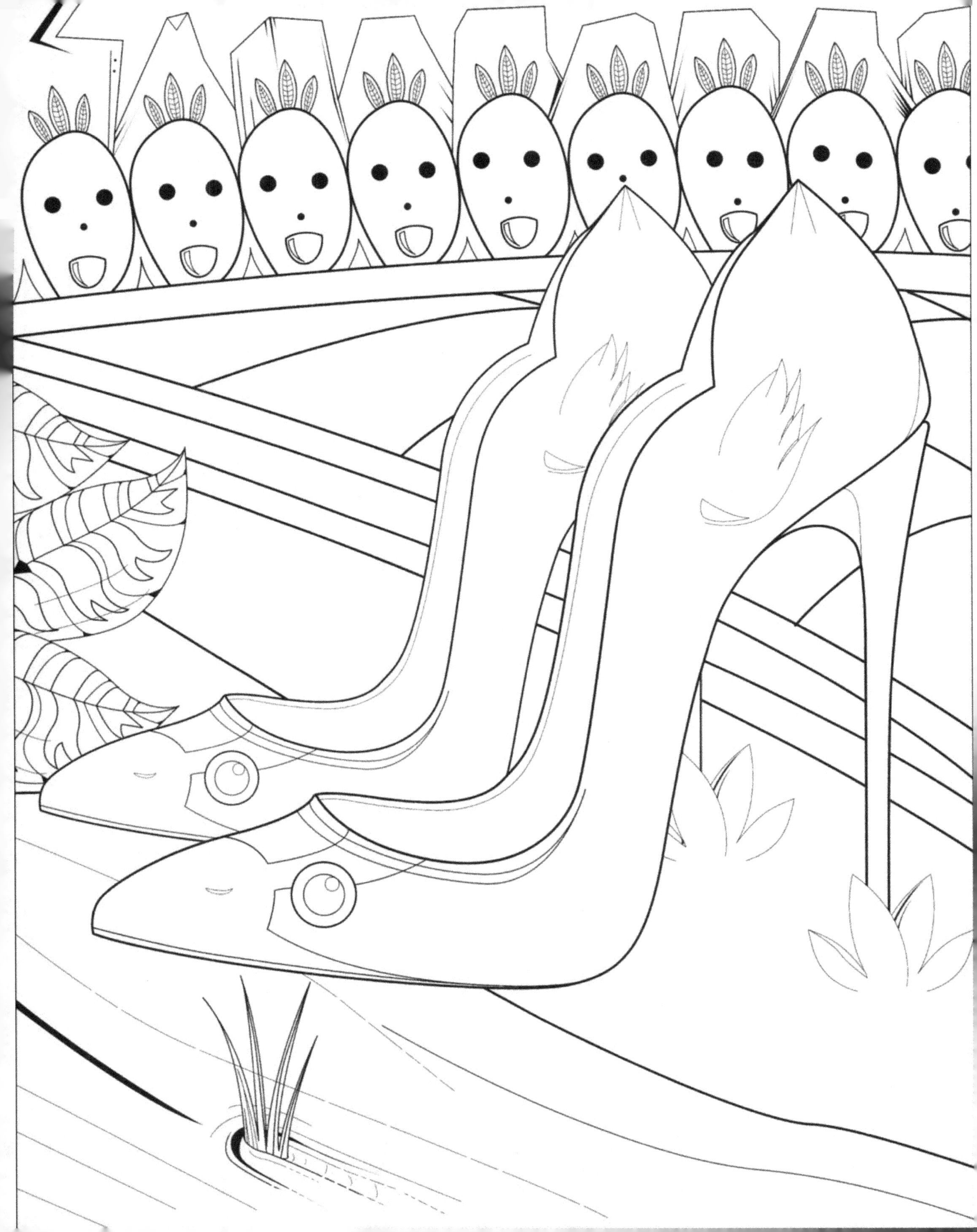

Stilettos and Boots

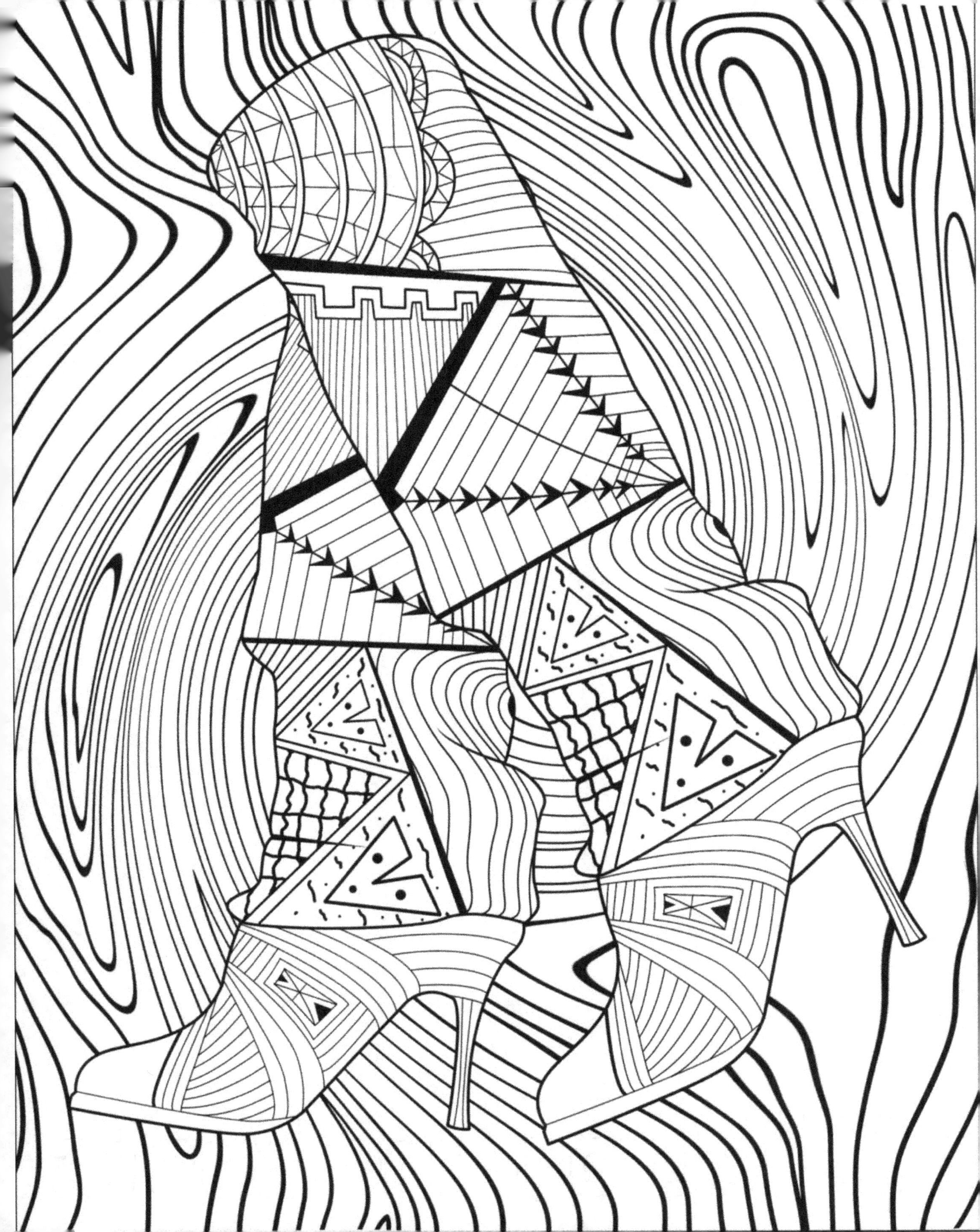

Stilettos and Boots

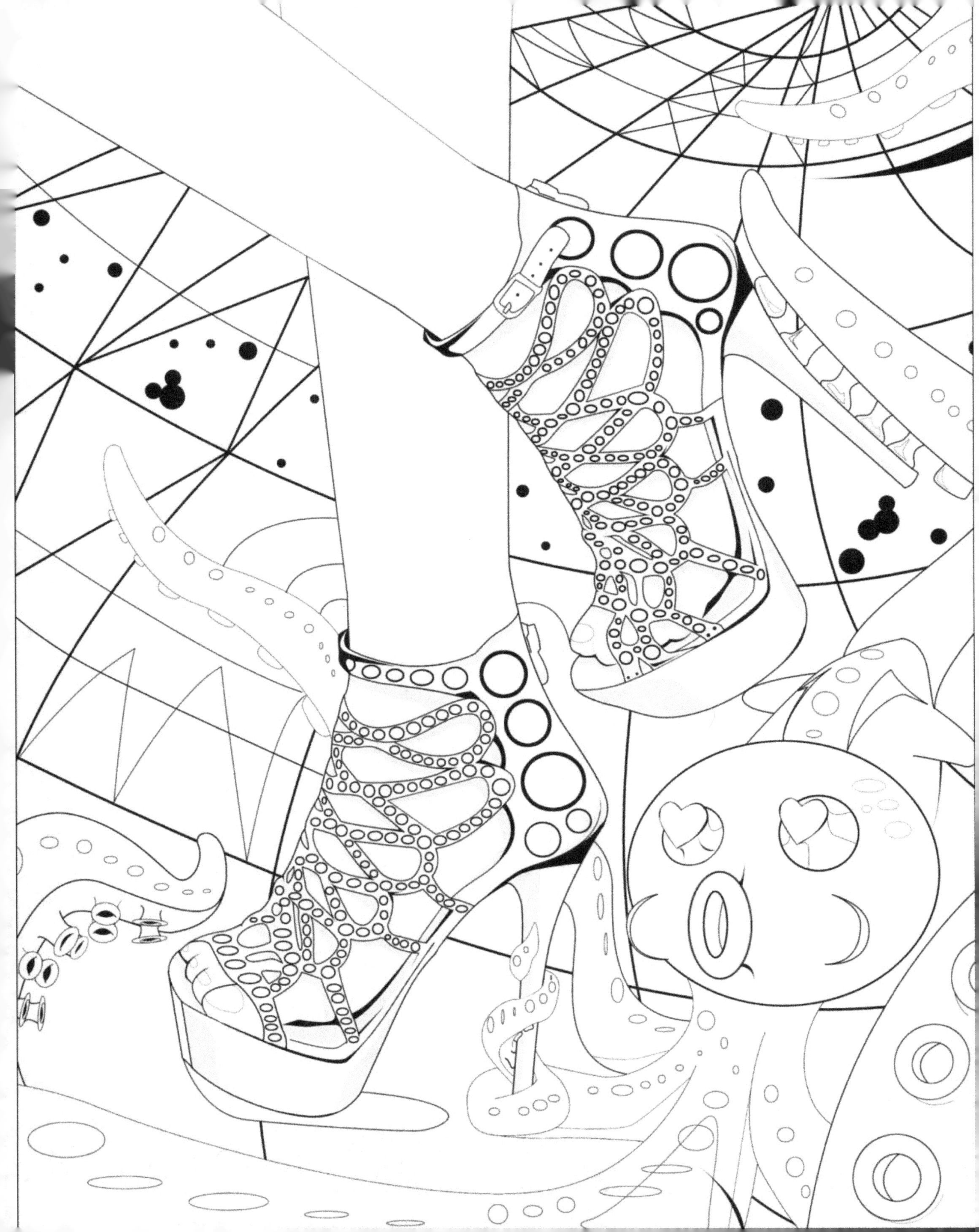

Stilettos and Boots

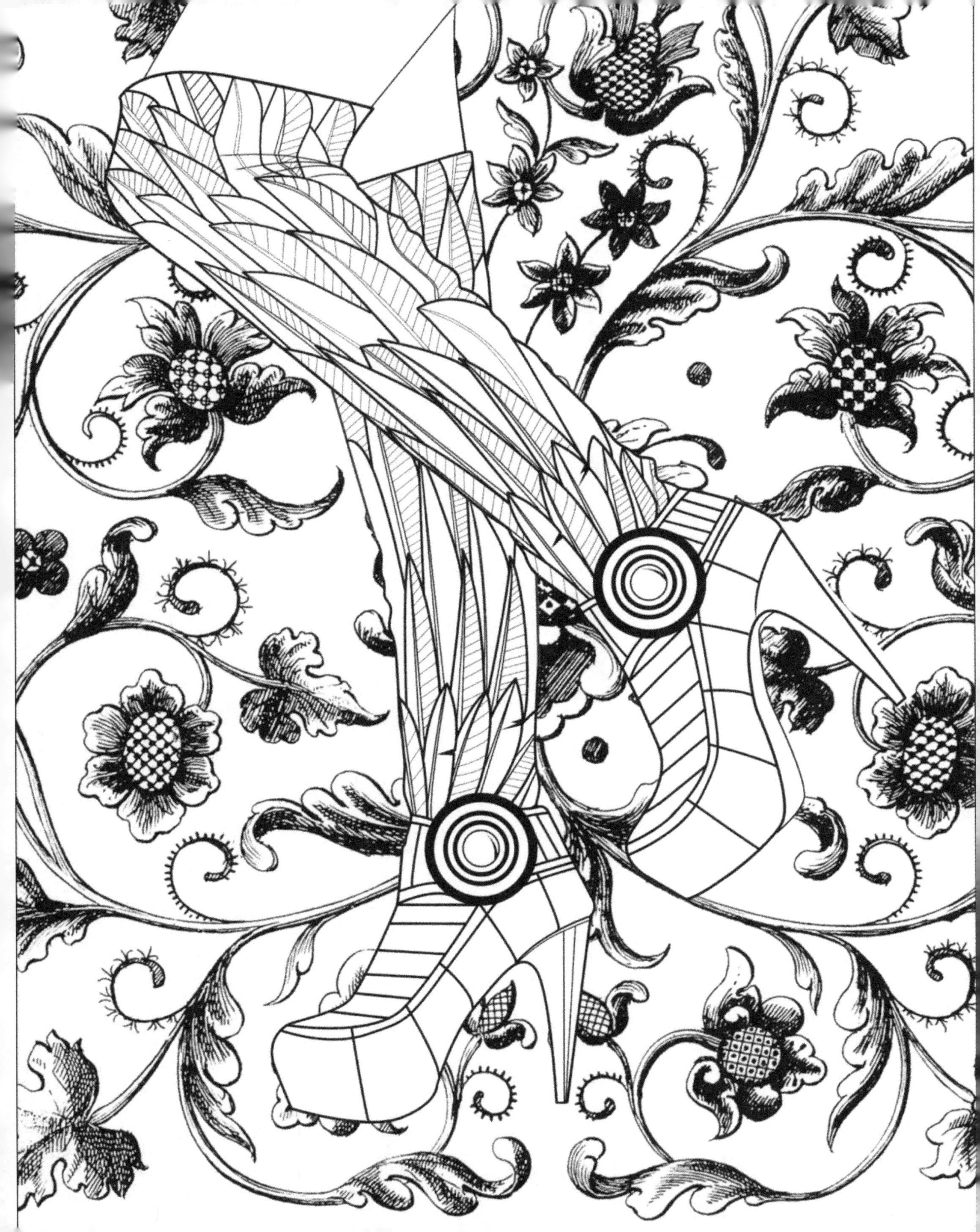

Stilettos and Boots

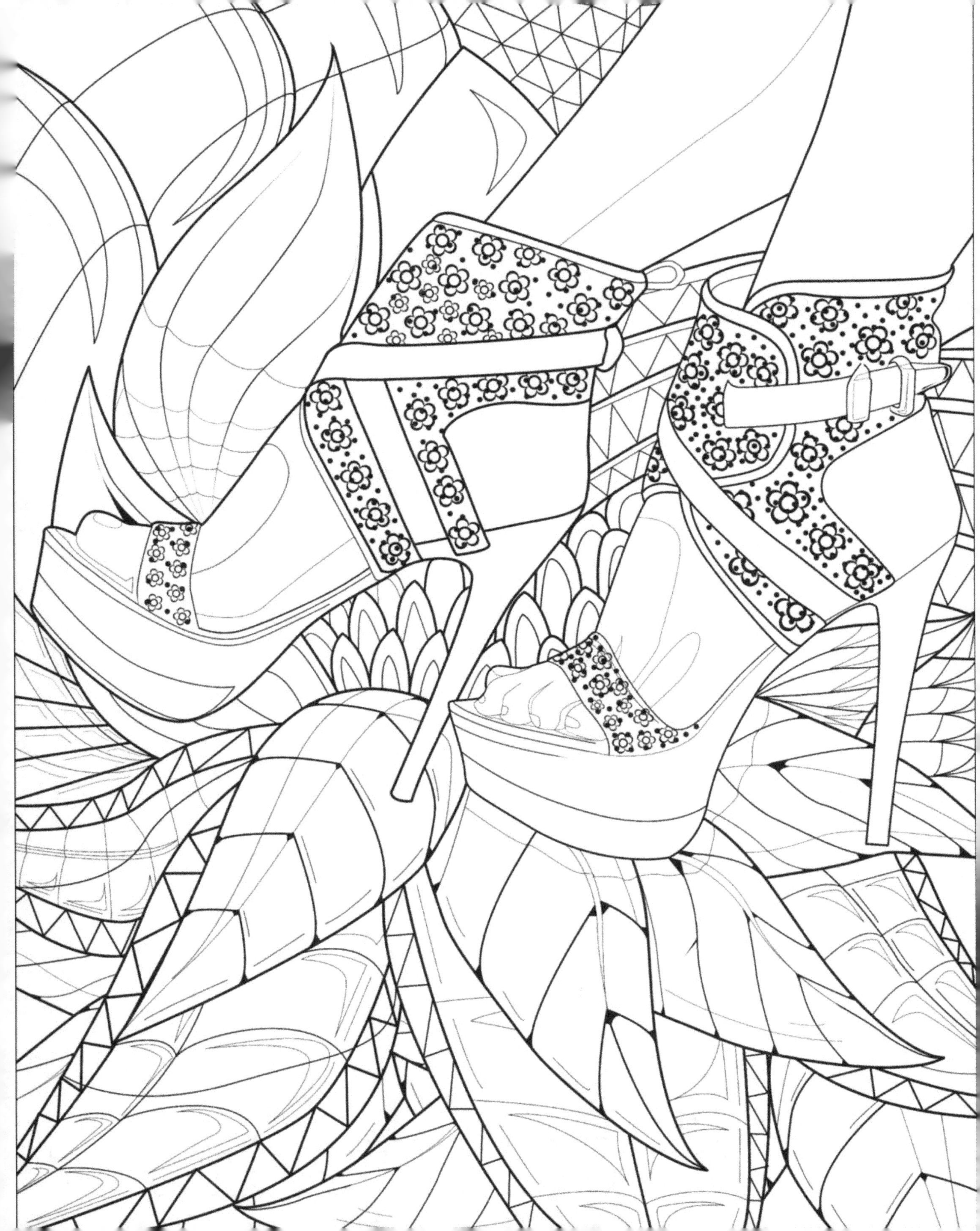

Stilettos and Boots

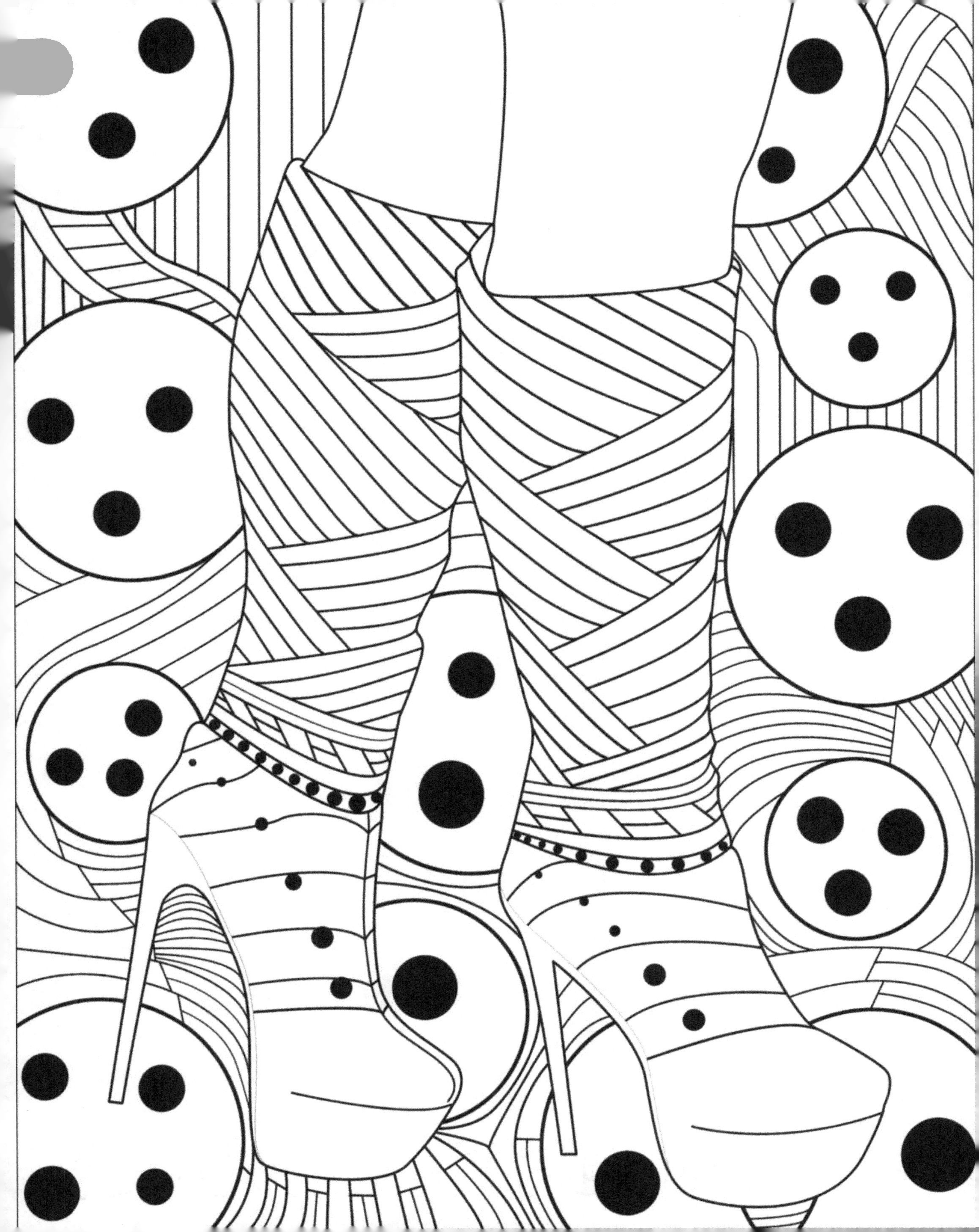

Stilettos and Boots

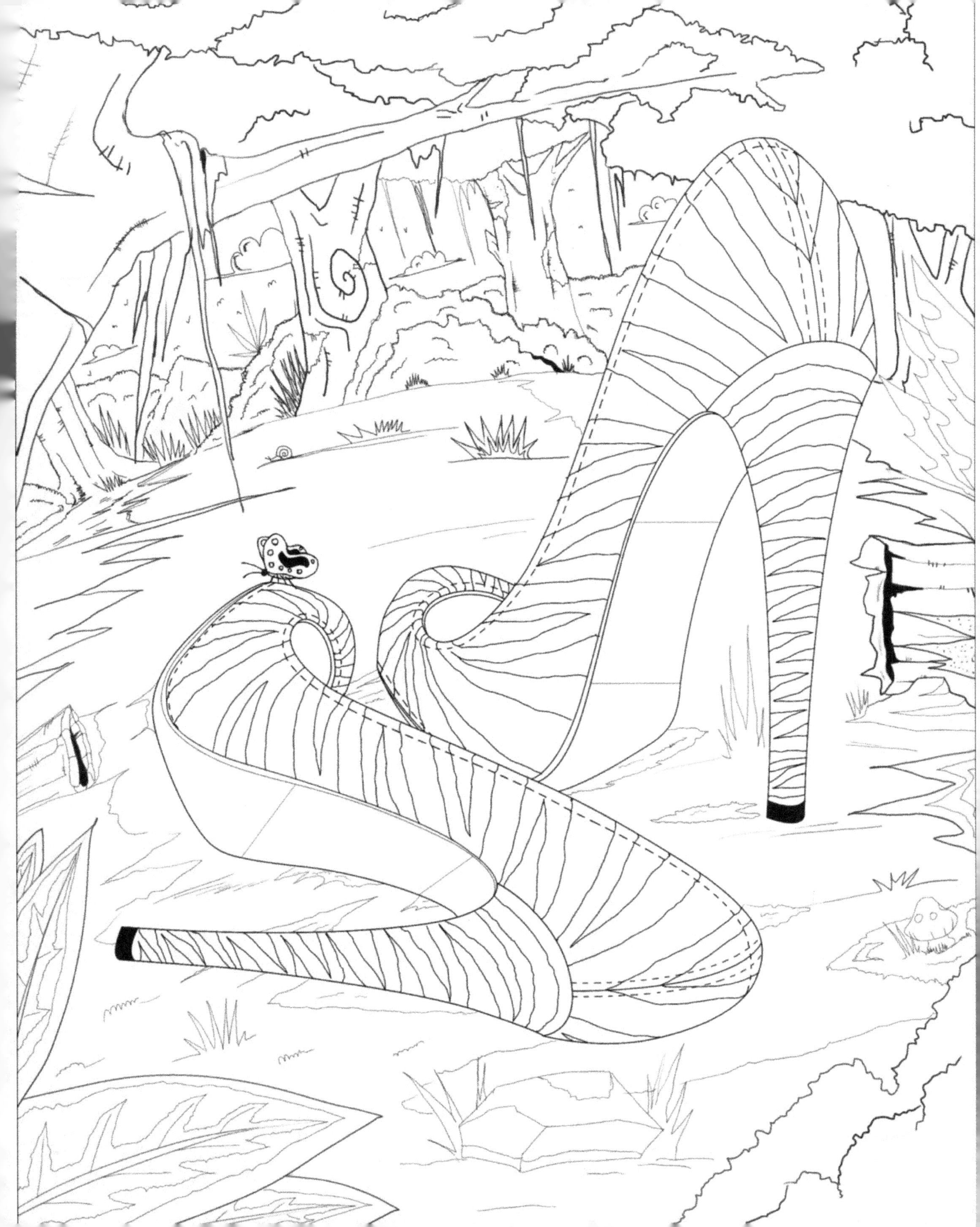

Stilettos and Boots

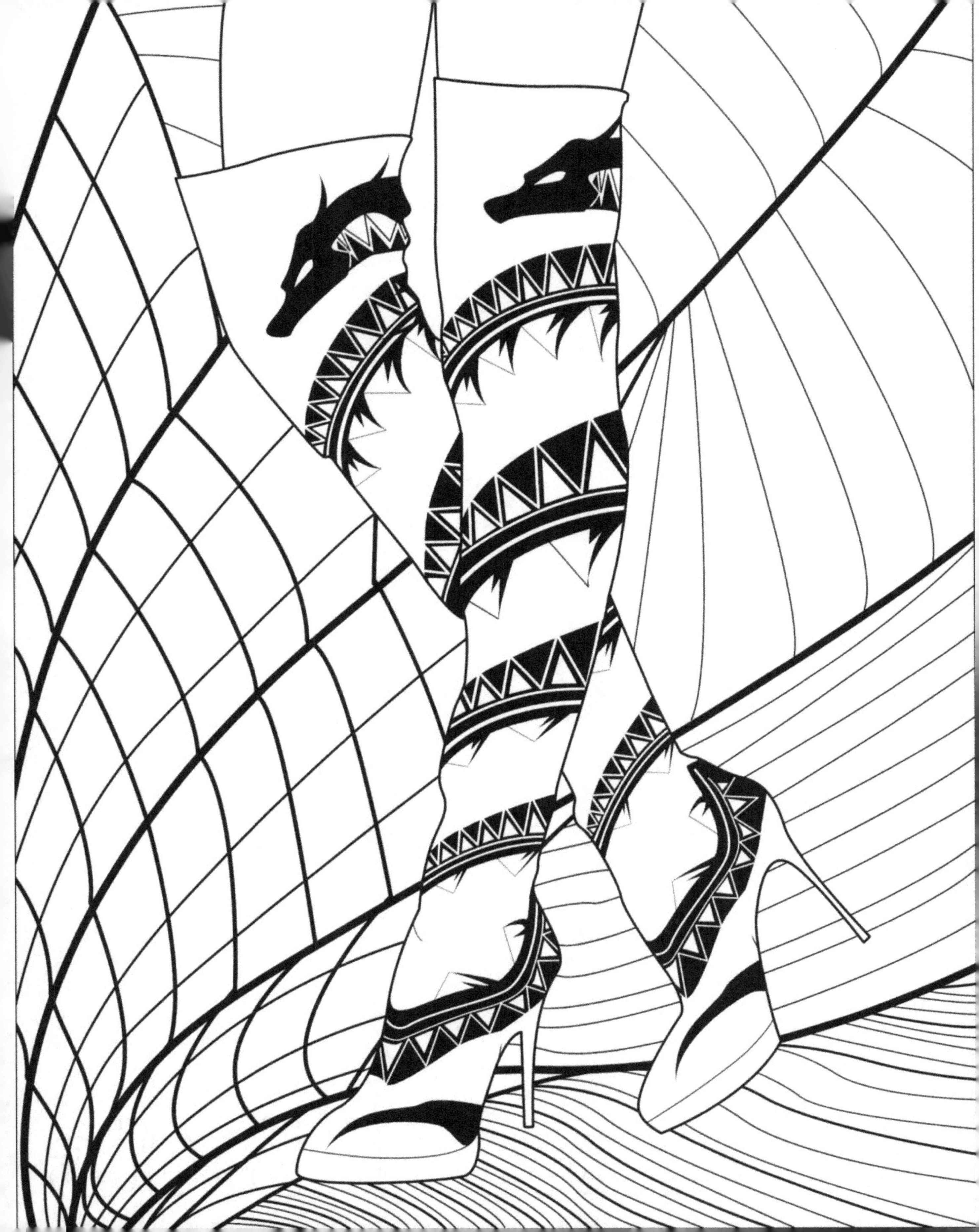

Stilettos and Boots

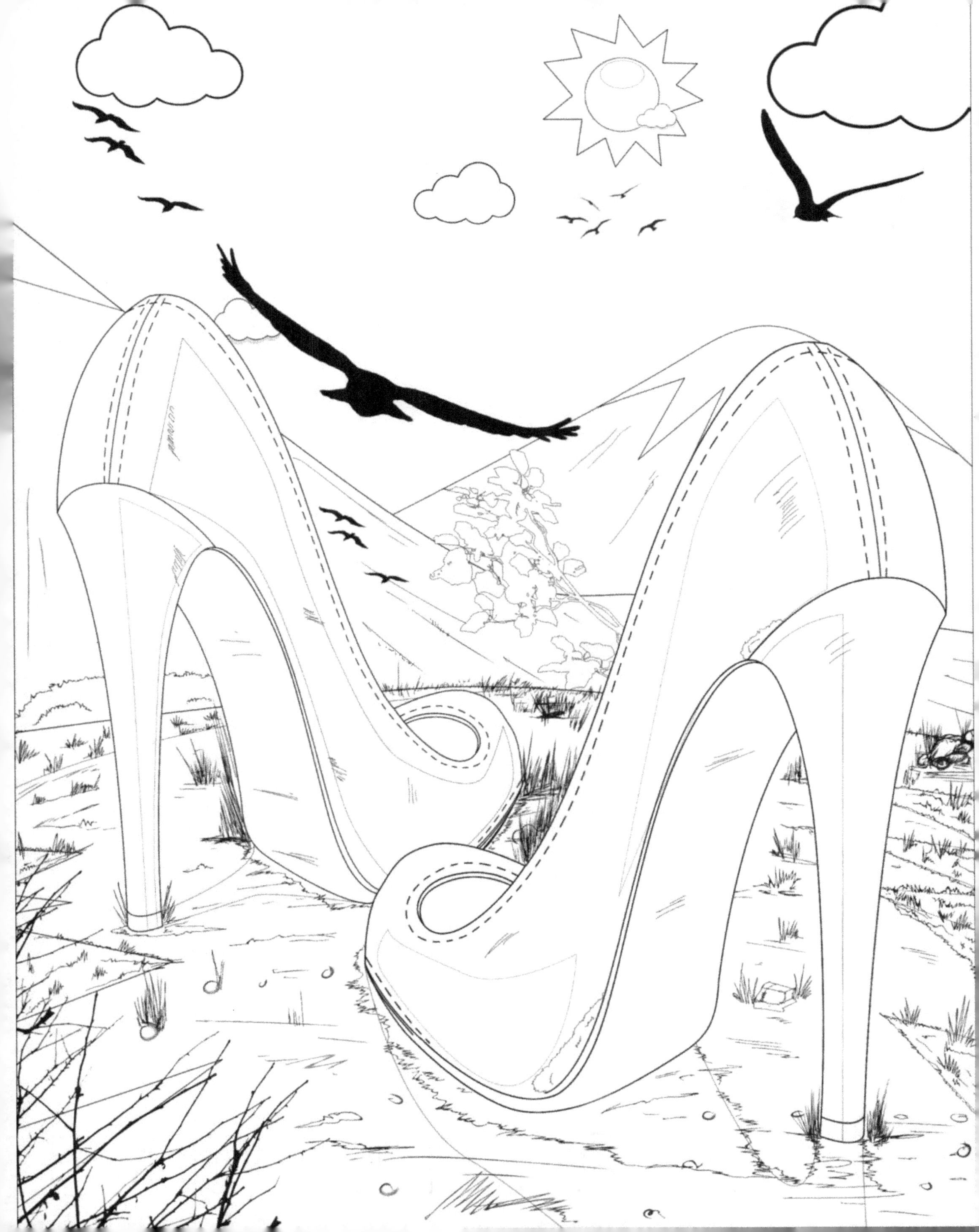

Stilettos and Boots

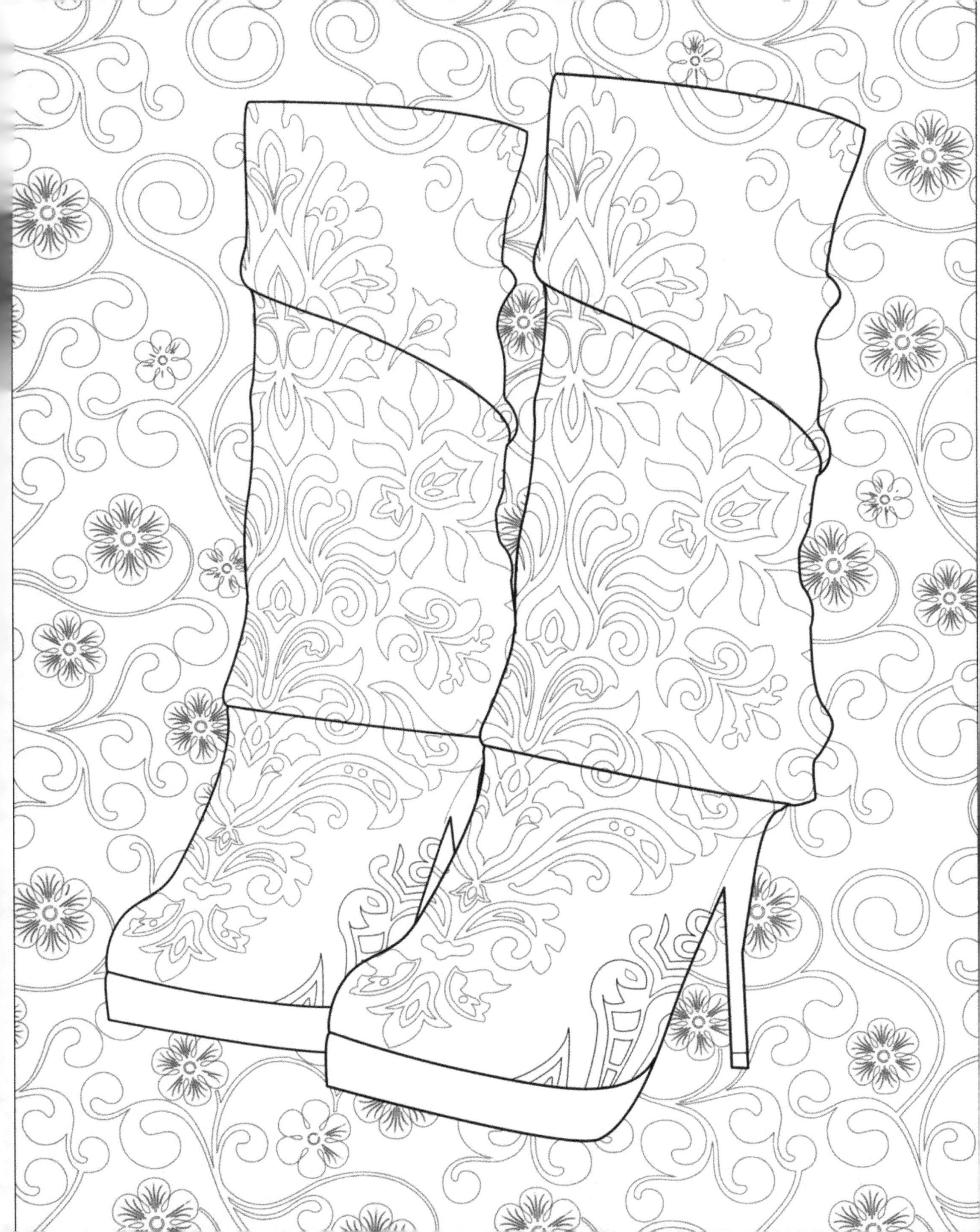

Stilettos and Boots

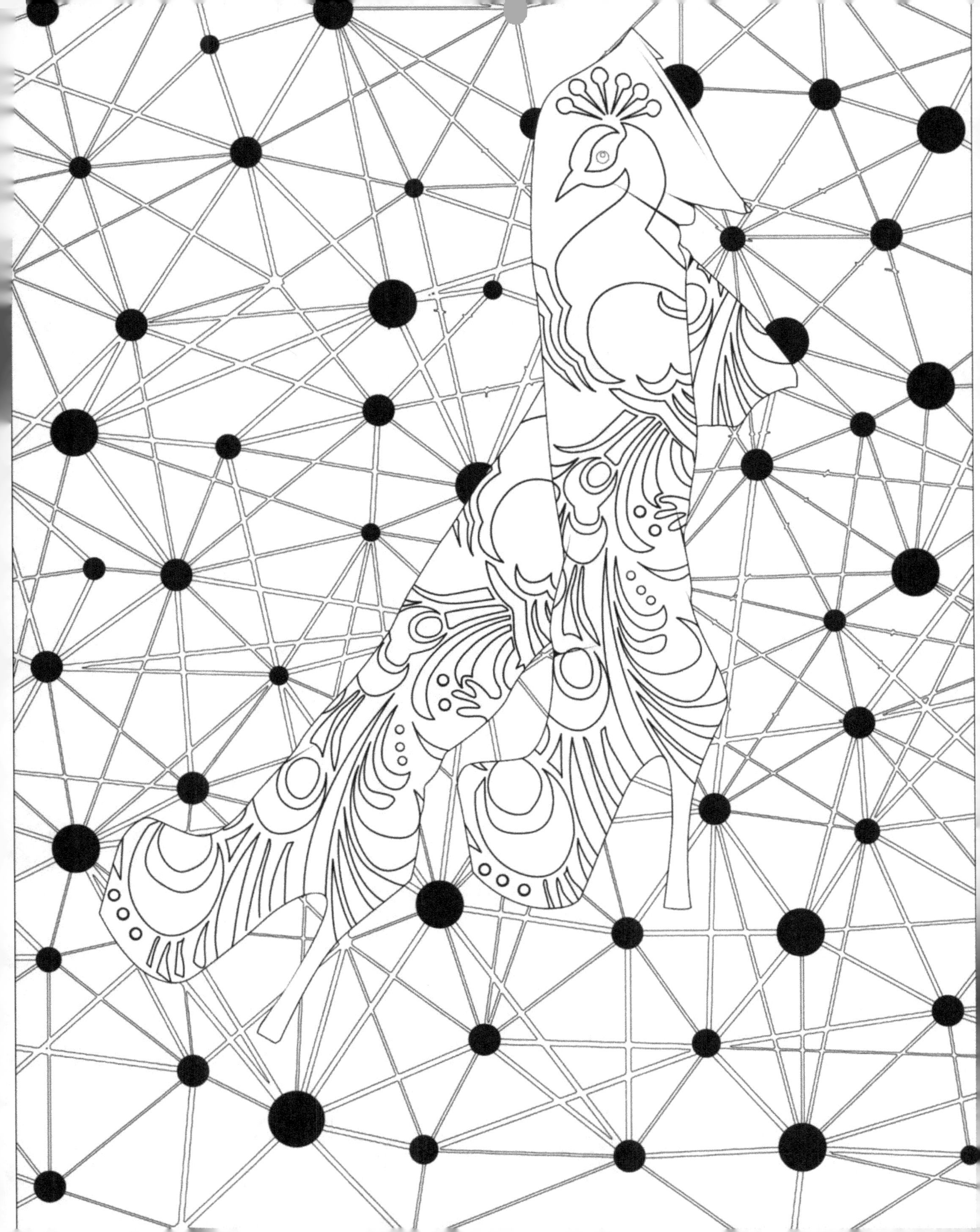

Stilettos and Boots

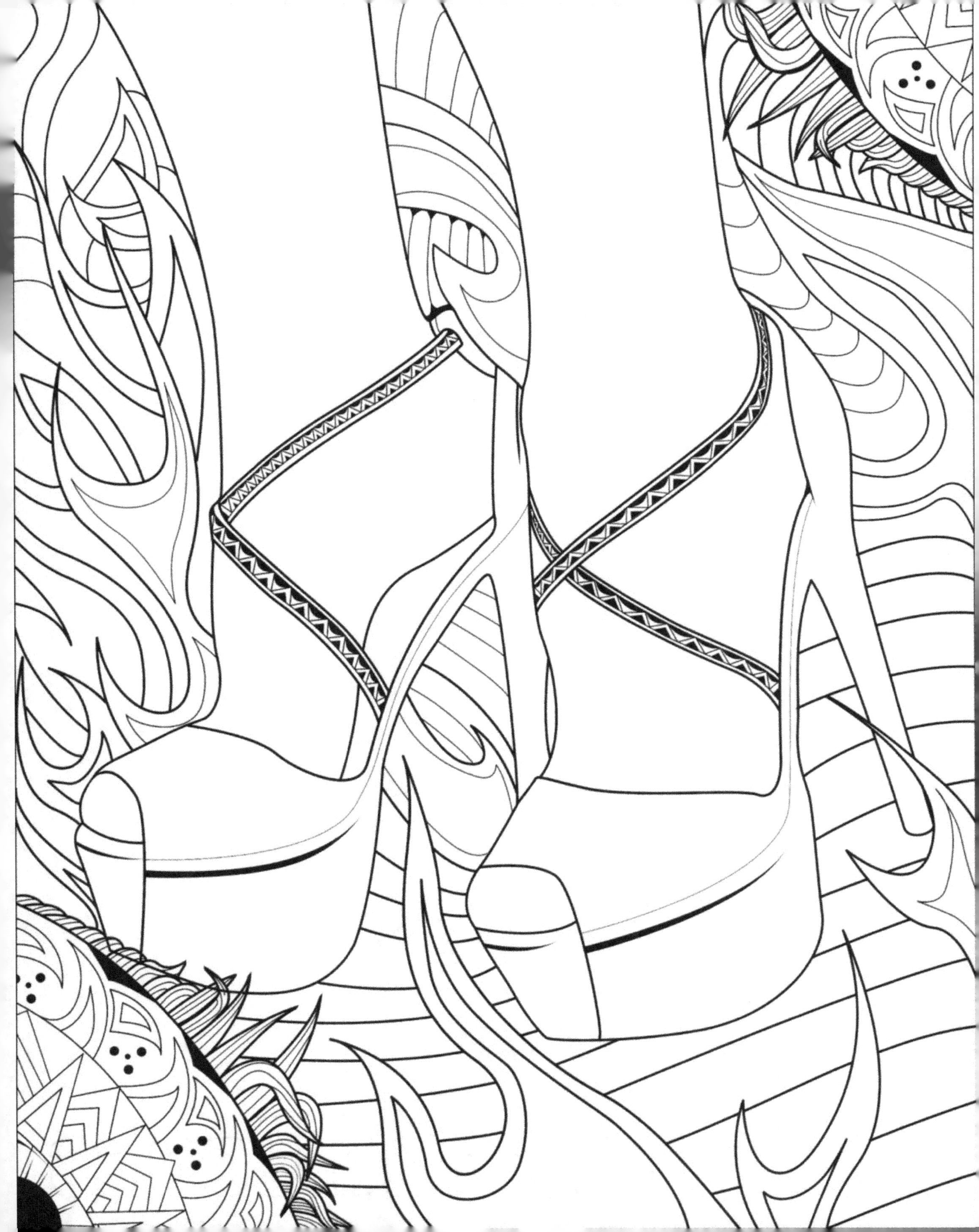

Stilettos and Boots

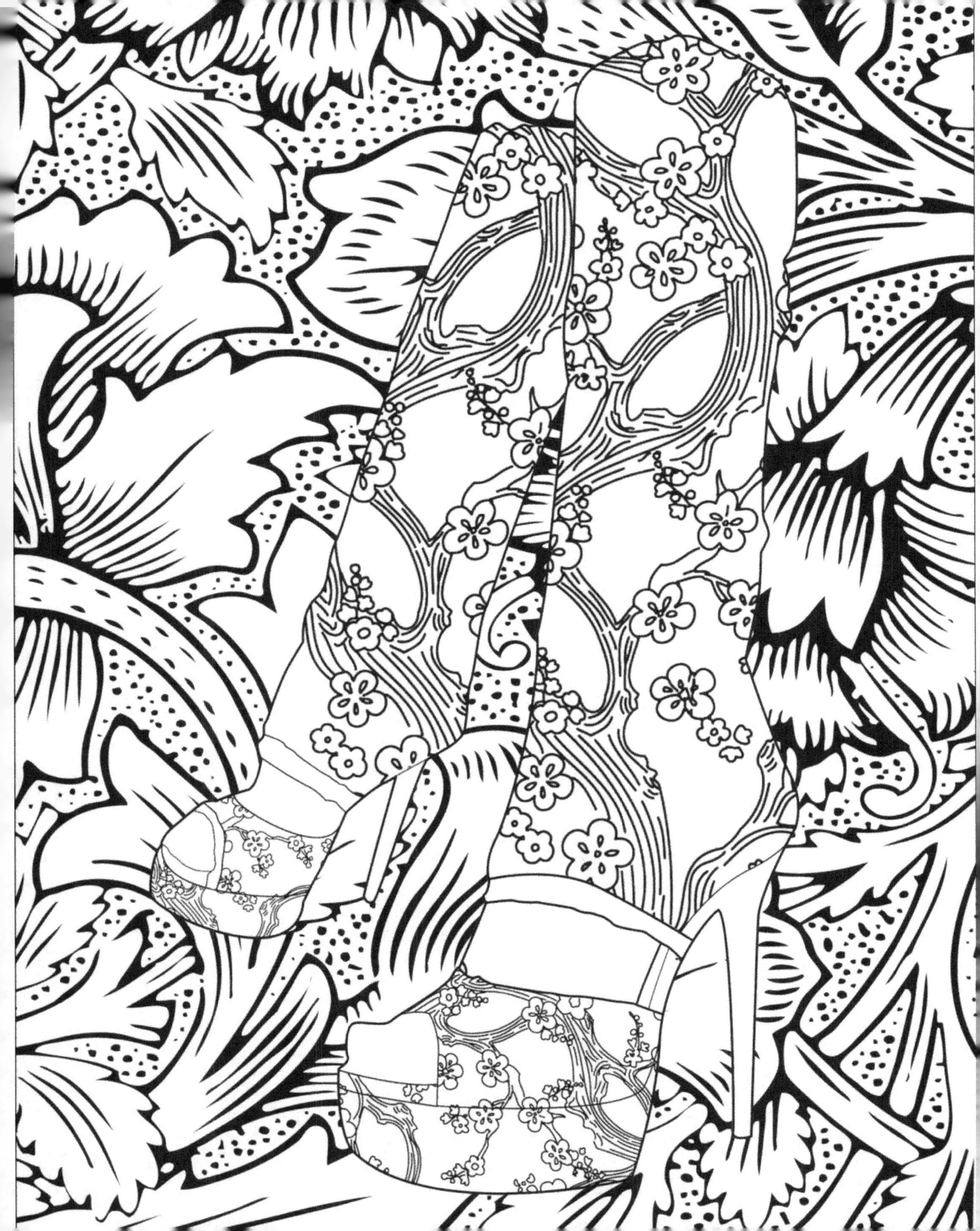

Stilettos and Boots

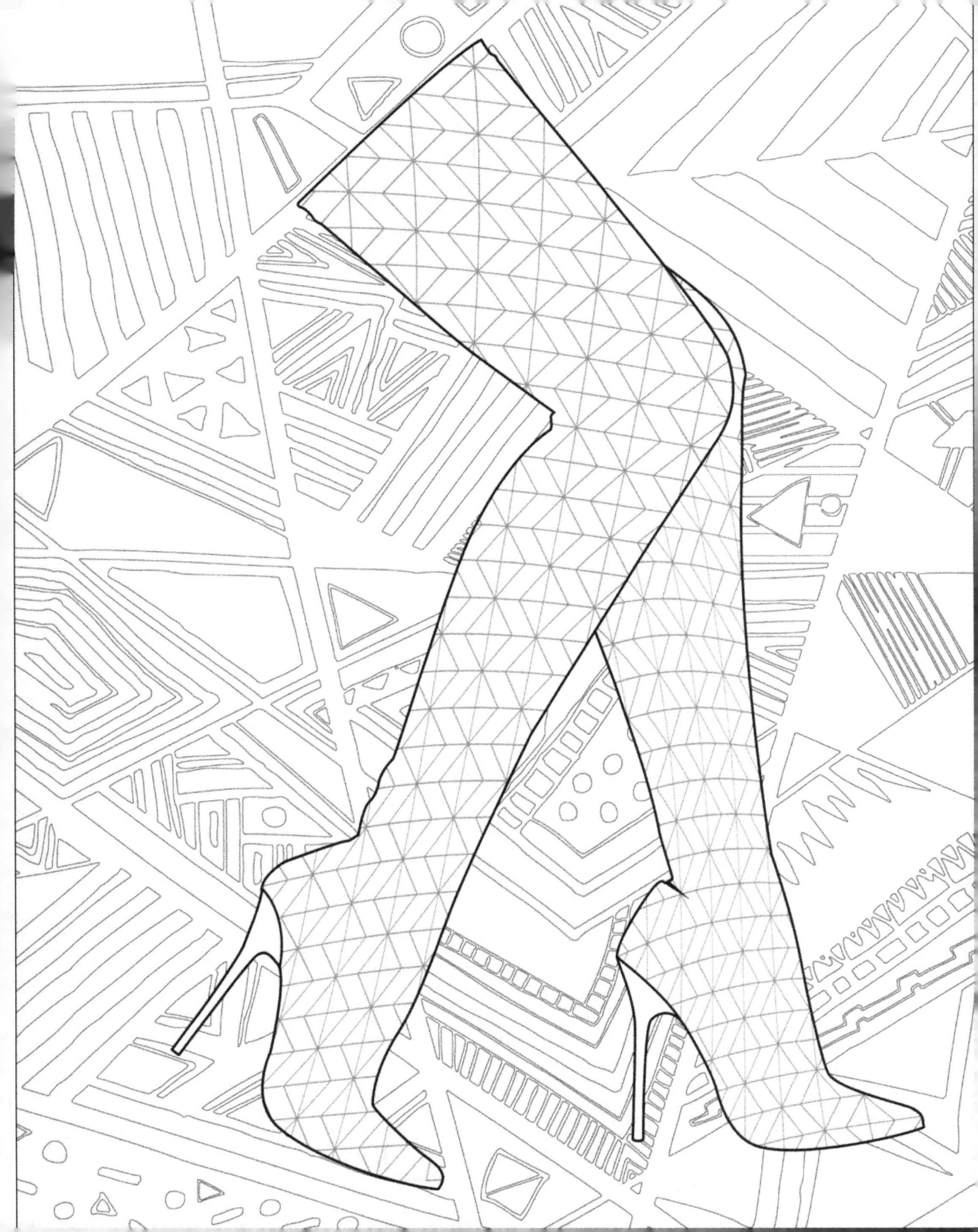

Stilettos and Boots

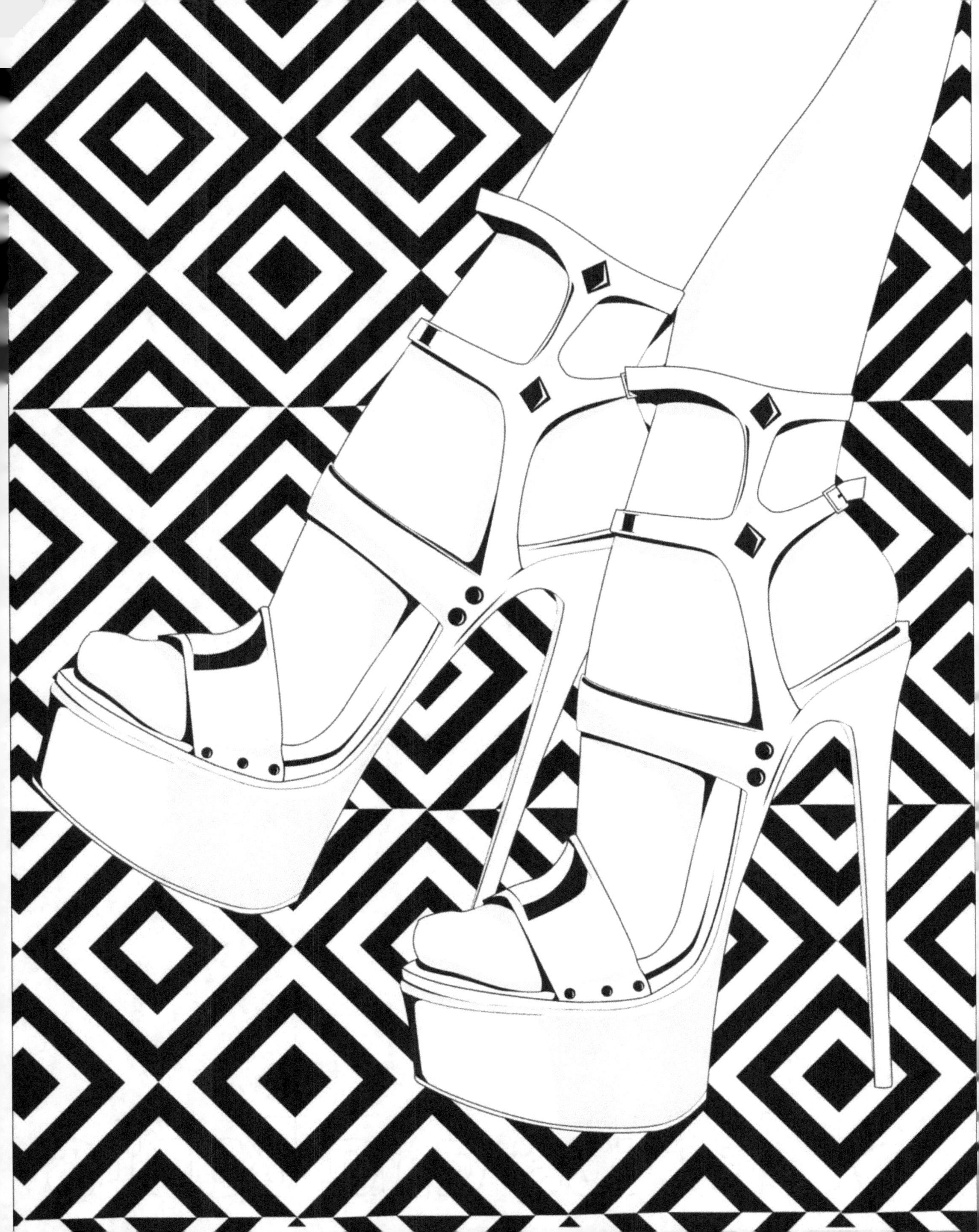

Stilettos and Boots

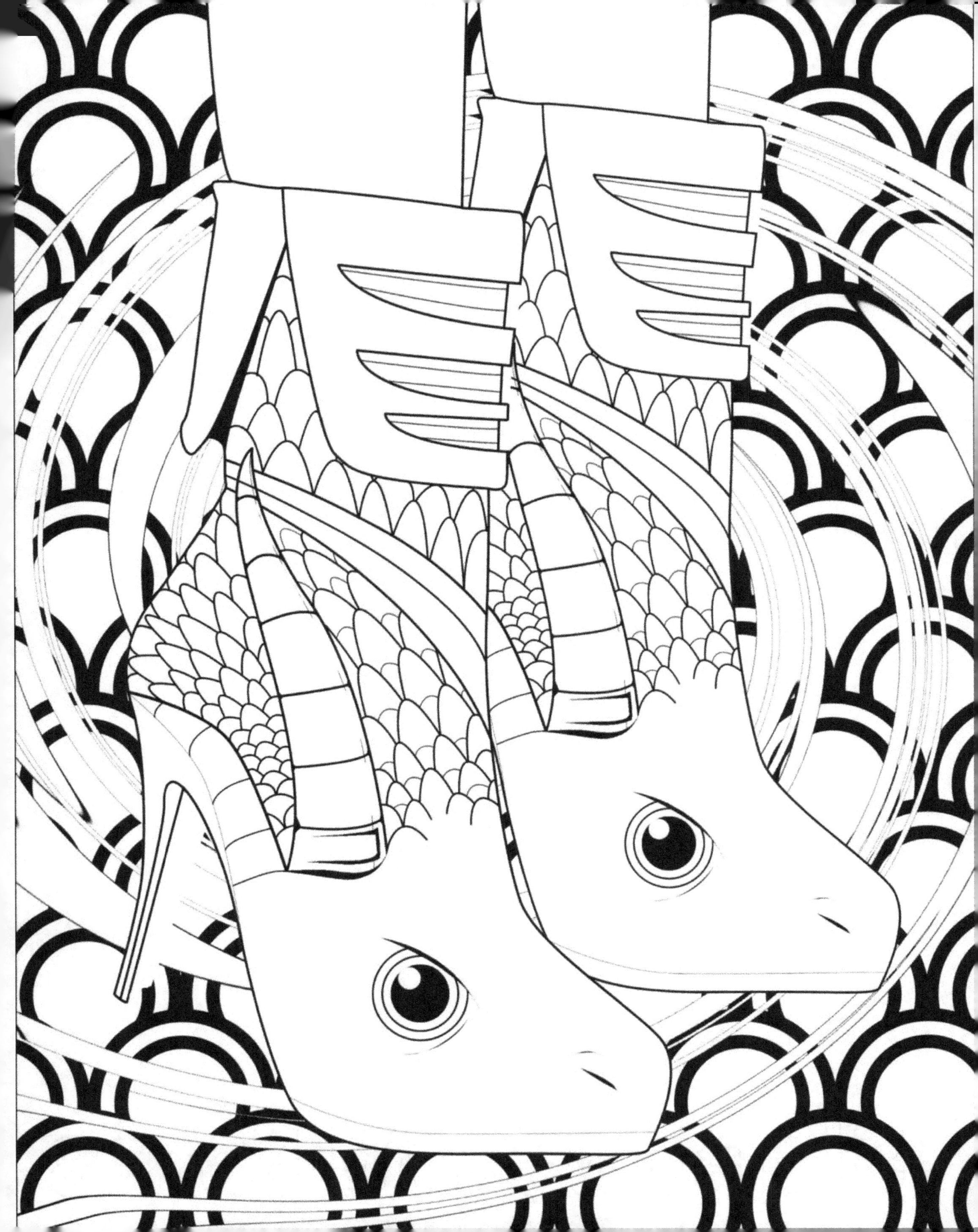

Stilettos and Boots

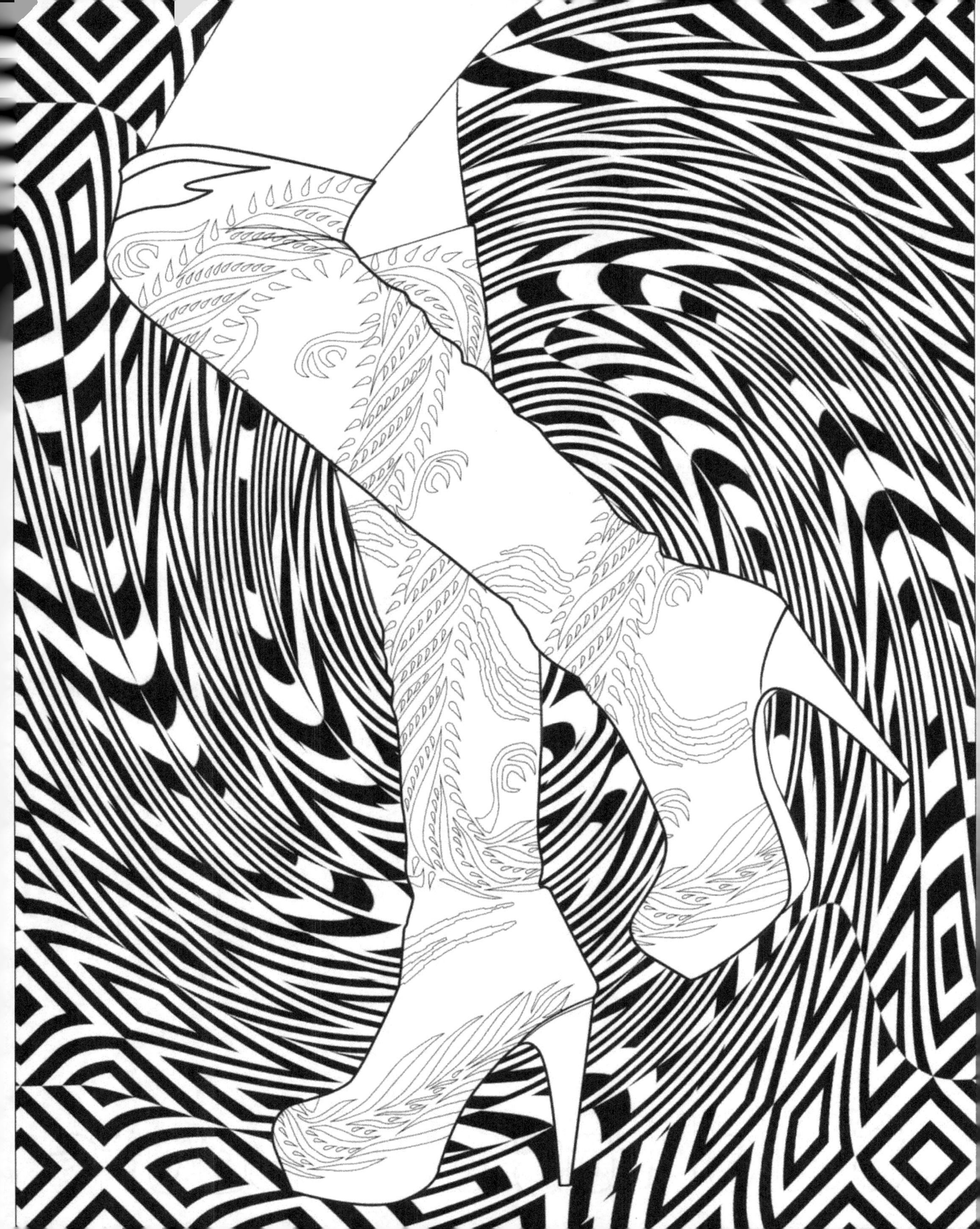

Stilettos and Boots

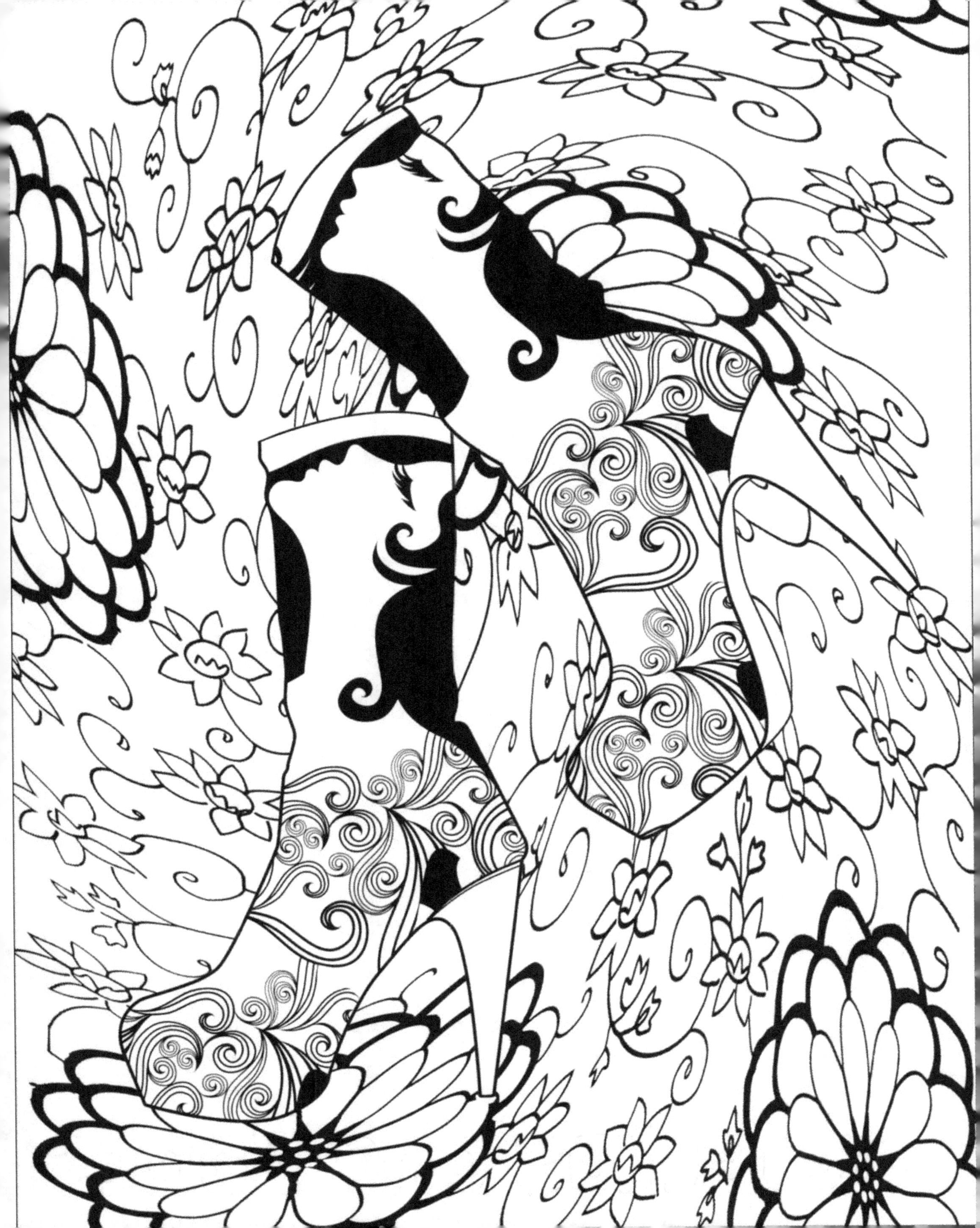

Stilettos and Boots

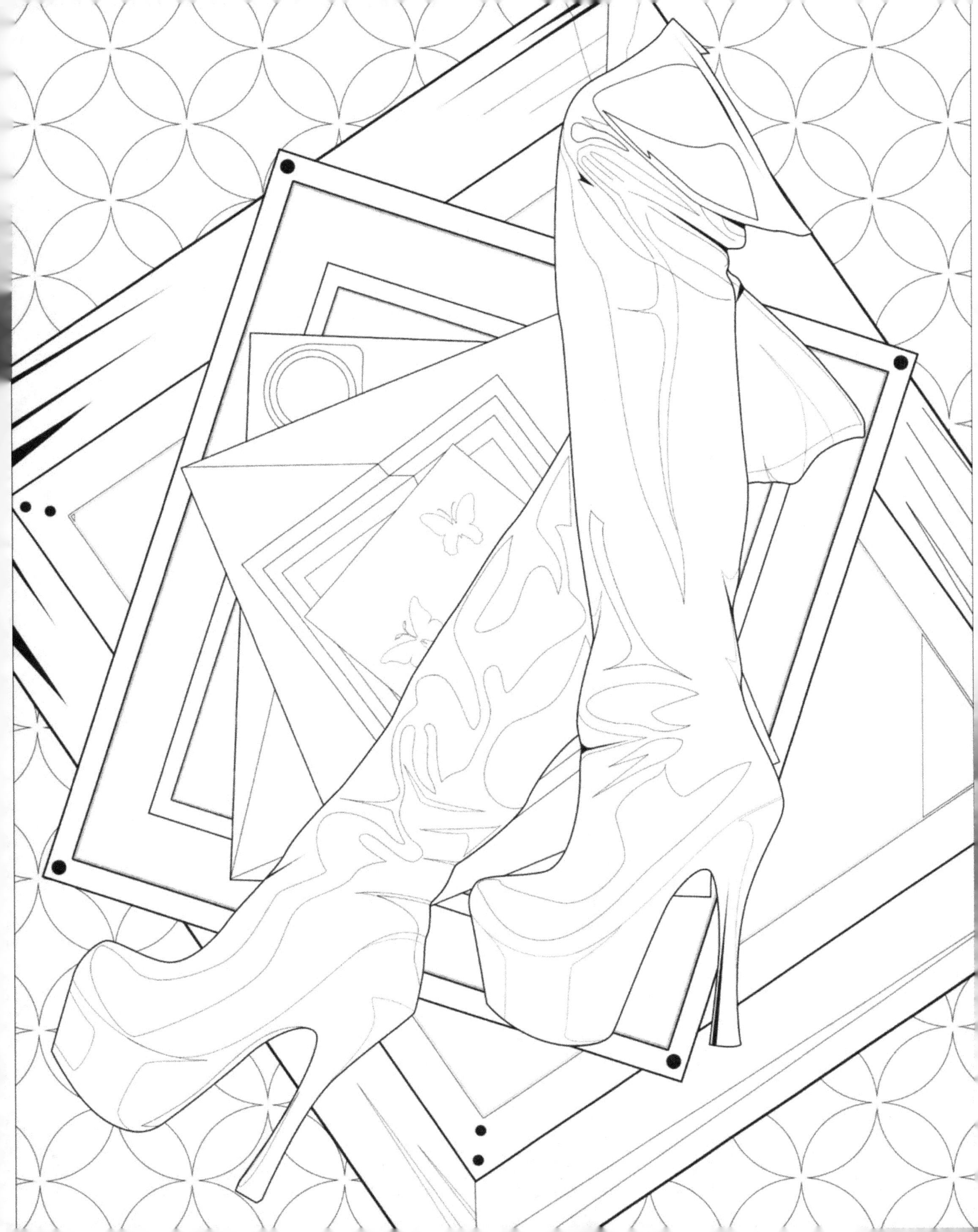

Stilettos and Boots

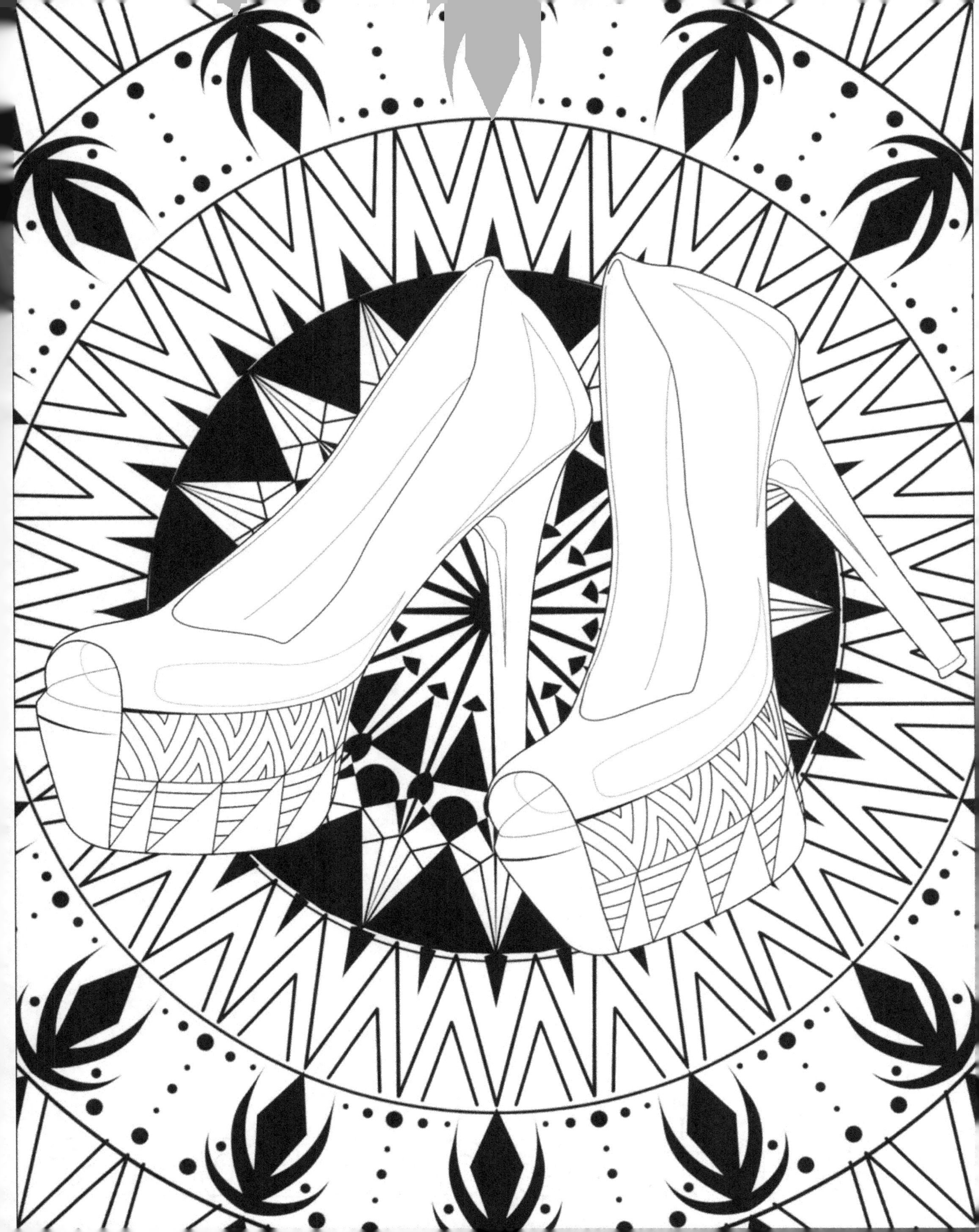

Stilettos and Boots

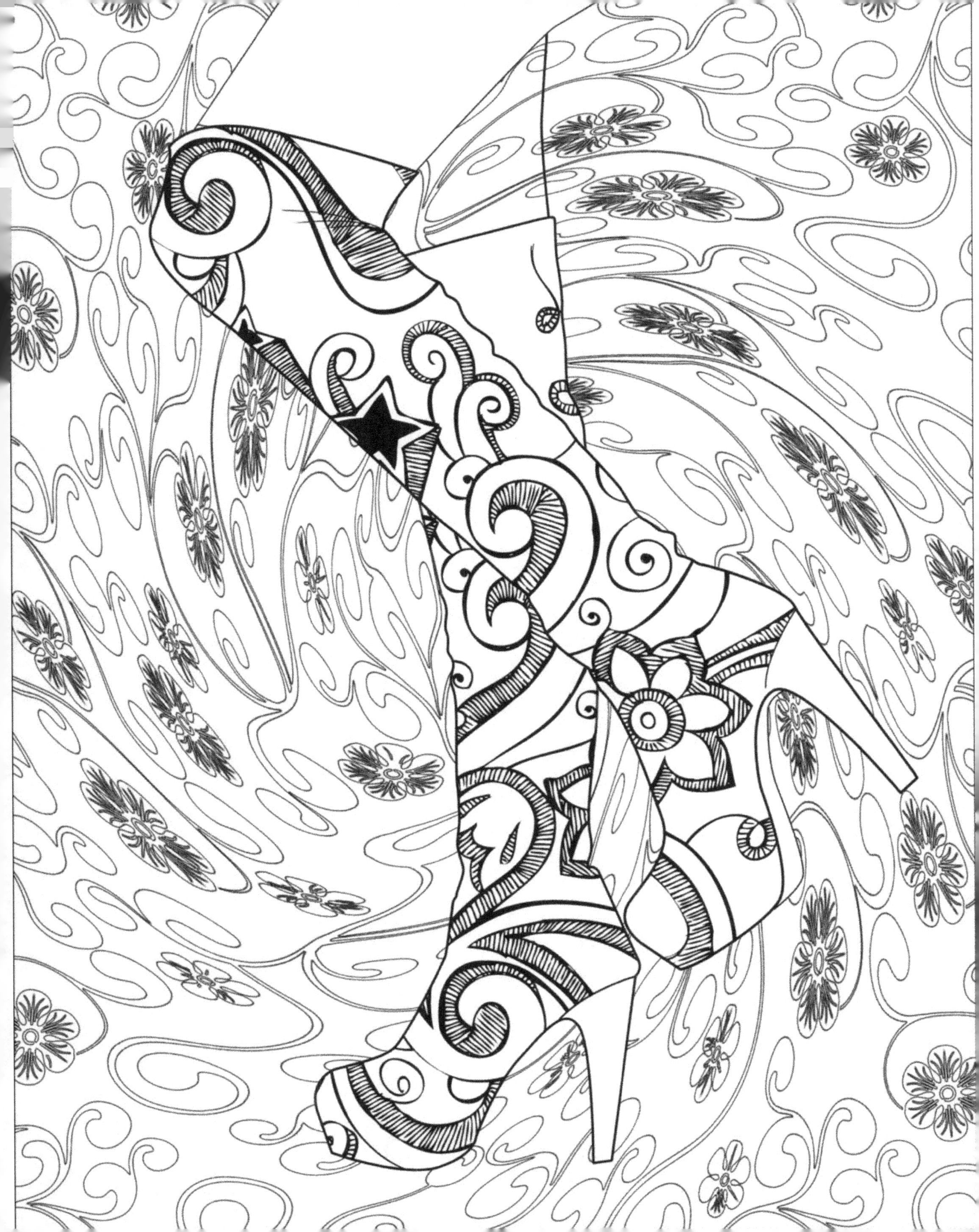

Stilettos and Boots

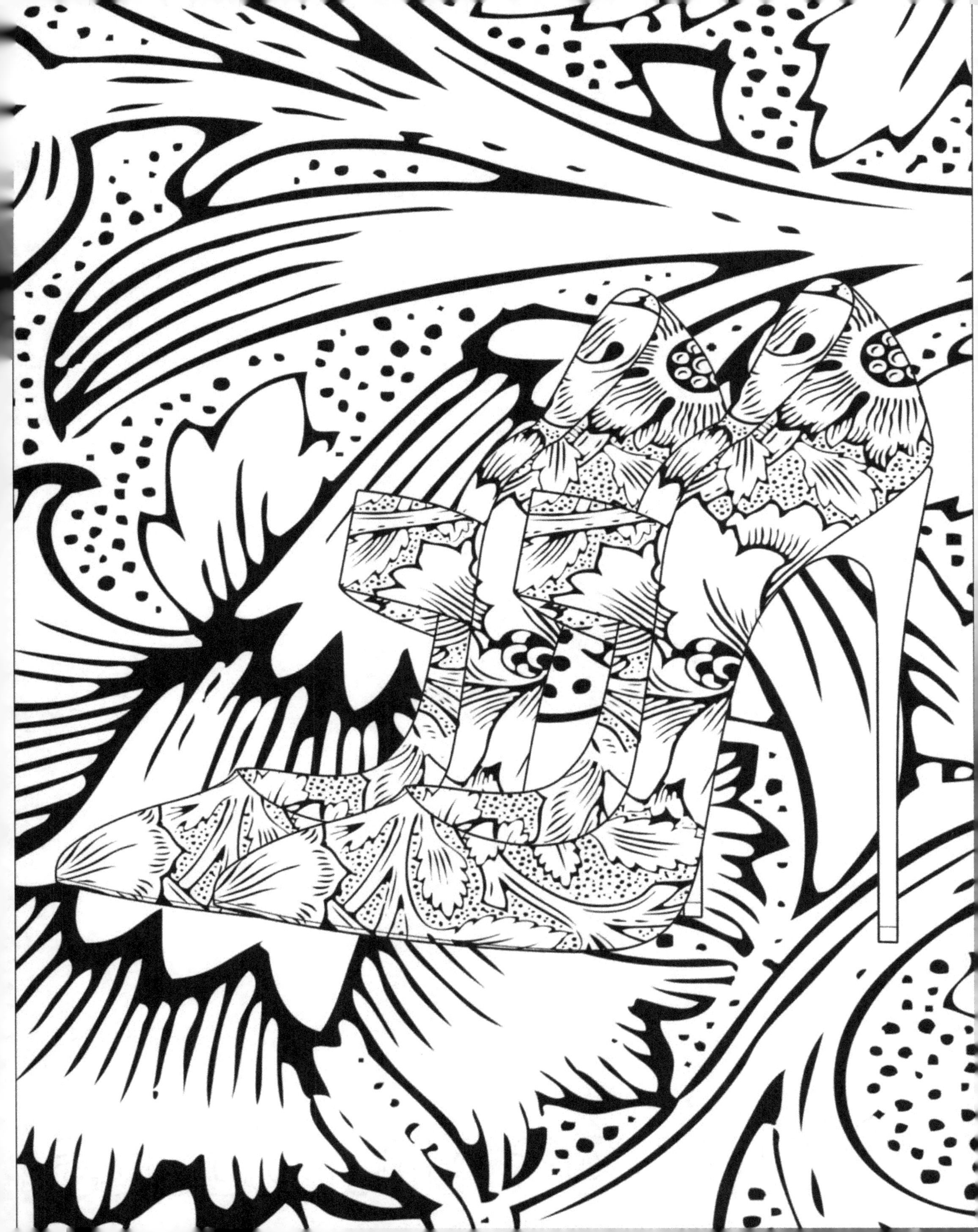

Stilettos and Boots

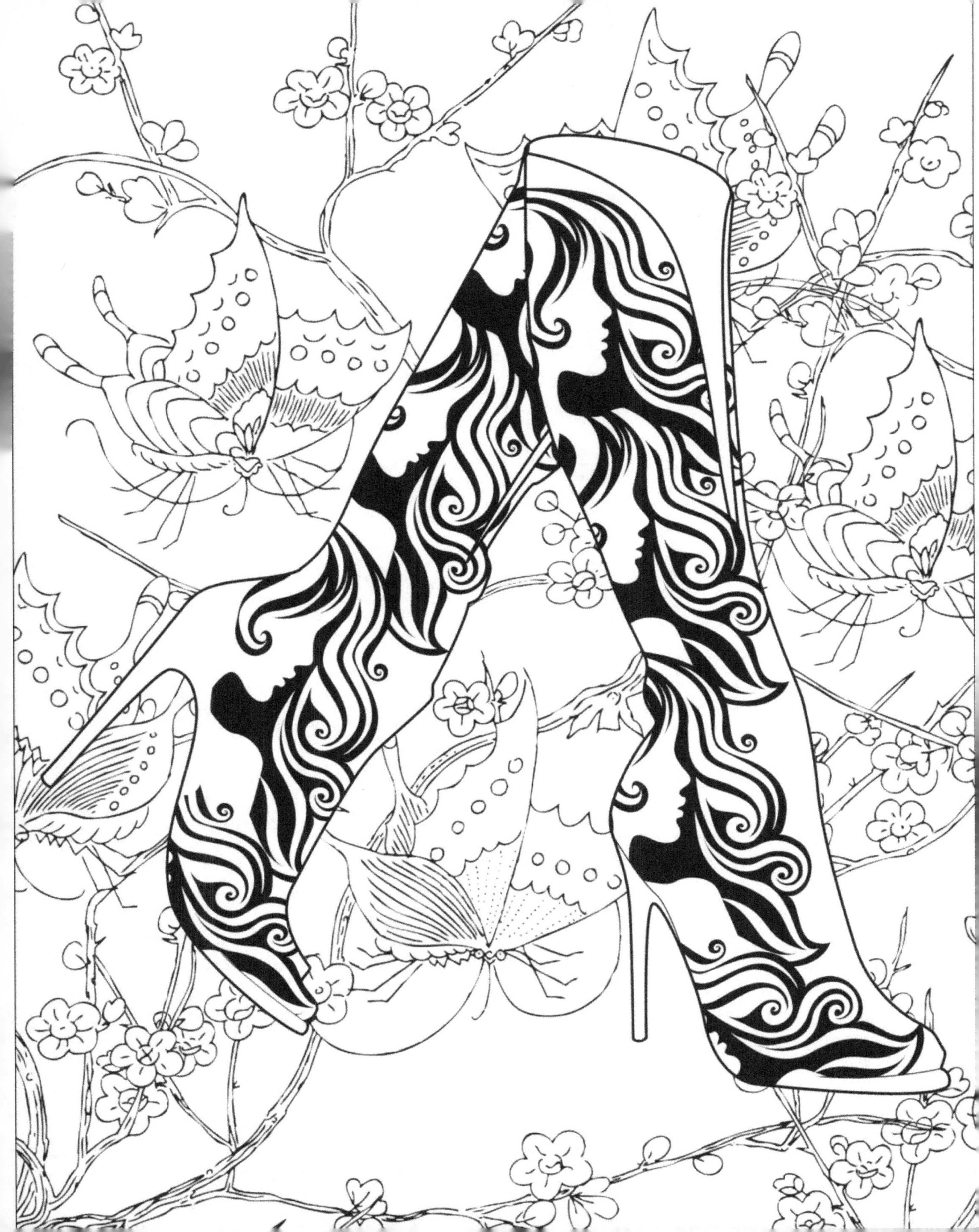

Stilettos and Boots

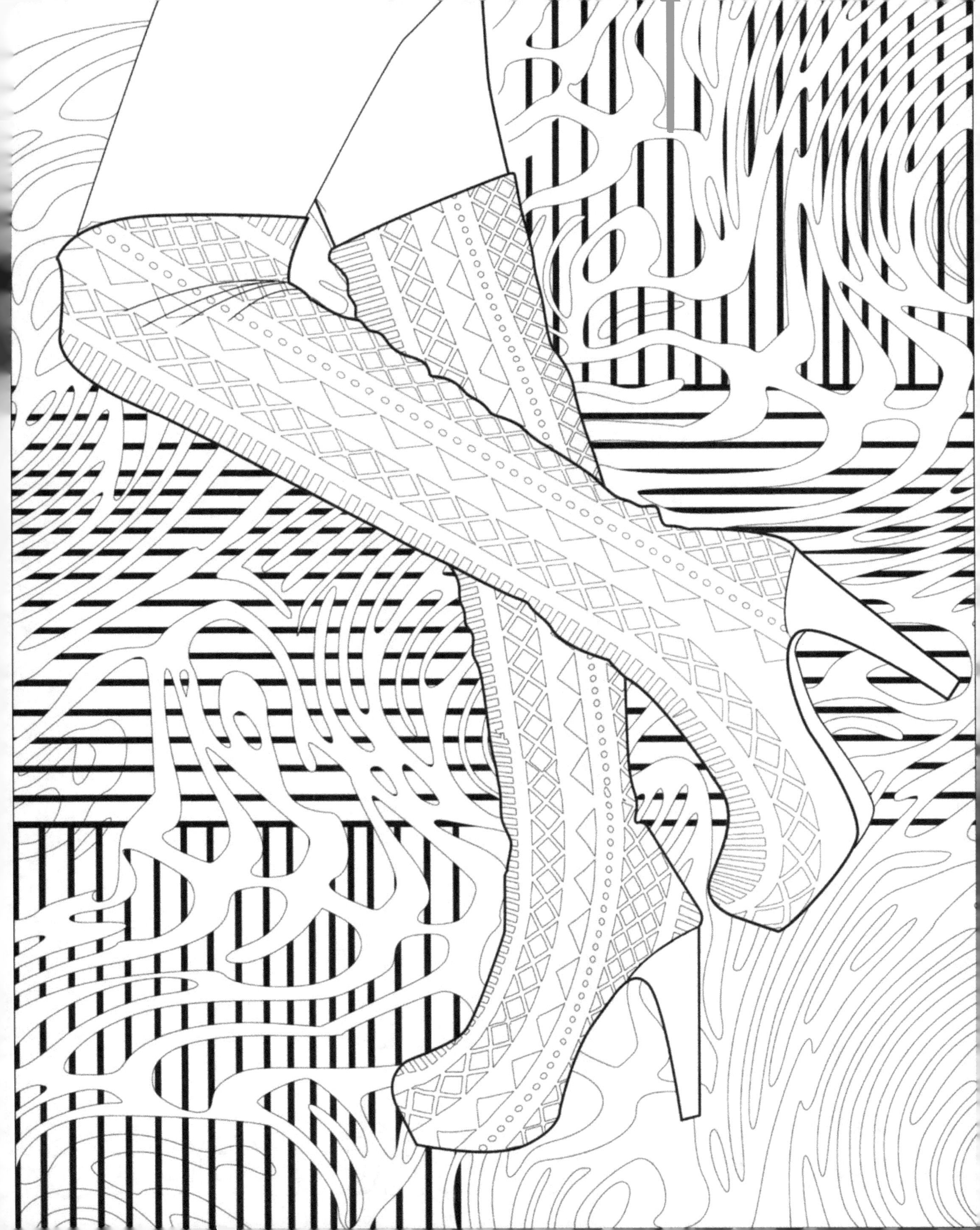

Stilettos and Boots

www.ingramcontent.com/pod-product-compliance
Lightning Source LLC
Chambersburg PA
CBHW080340030726
47594CB00012B/4089